P37/3

EXECUTIVES
UNDER
PRESSURE

EXECUTIVES UNDER PRESSURE

A Psychological Study

Judi Marshall
and
Cary L. Cooper

First published 1979 by
THE MACMILLAN PRESS LTD
London and Basingstoke
Associated companies in Delhi
Dublin Hong Kong Johannesburg Lagos
Melbourne New York Singapore Tokyo

Typeset in Great Britain at
The Pitman Press, *Bath*

Printed in Great Britain by offset lithography by
Billing & Sons Ltd, Guildford, London and Worcester

British Library Cataloguing in Publication Data

Marshall, Judi
    Executives under pressure.
    1. Executives   2. Stress (Physiology)
    3. Stress (Psychology)
    I. Title   II. Cooper, Cary Lynn
    158.7   HF5548.8

    ISBN 0-333-23889-3

This volume is dedicated to the managers and their wives who kindly made up our sample, and to the 'Steering Group'

Contents

Preface

In our previous book, *Understanding Executive Stress*, we discussed some of the potential sources of pressure on managers at work. These ranged from individual and organisational stressors to pressures acting on executives as a result of the inevitable conflicts created by the interface of work and family life. Much of this was speculative, based on research work carried out on other occupational groupings (e.g. engineers, clerical staff, etc.), and predominantly by occupational health researchers (i.e. medics). In addition, it relied on the *descriptive* work of many company medical officers and others (e.g. personnel) concerned with organisational well-being and health. Much of this groundwork has provided us with the impetus to carry out a full-scale research project into the social psychological sources of managerial stress. This book describes our study, which was carried out with the full cooperation of a large sample of managers and (some of) their wives. We hope that you will feel, as we do, that this work goes a step further toward providing information necessary to take the most appropriate action to *manage* stress at work and within organisations.

Manchester

1977

J.M.
C.L.C.

1 Introduction: Costs of Stress

Stress is a topical subject; there is no escaping its increasing coverage in both popular and academic literature. It has been suggested that this 'popularity' may be because, as a concept, it integrates several previously distinct fields of social science study (McGrath, 1970), or, more cynically, that it is the result of a 'bandwagon effect' (Appley, 1964). A simpler and more easily supported possibility is that it is a topic of direct relevance to a large proportion of the inhabitants of today's Western industrial world (as the release of tension, which typically accompanies its open discussion convincingly shows). Public and government concern is increasing as the short- and long-term effects of stress for the individual, his family, the company he works for and even the national economy are being realised. Let us look briefly at the 'accounting' that can be done at each of these levels.

For the individual, stress means 'human suffering' – short-term discomfort and unhappiness, but with the possibility of long-term disease. There is a substantial body of occupational health literature which documents those effects of relevance in the workplace (e.g. McGhee, 1963; Webber, 1966; Pettigrew, 1972; Kenton, 1974) – anxiety, inability to concentrate, irritability, minor physical ailments, etc. Hinkle (1973) is amongst the majority who believe that these initial signs and symptoms lead on to longer-term, incapacitating diseases:

> Thus the potential magnitude of the effects (of reactions to the environment) appears to be as great as the effects which can be produced by any other influence upon these processes, not even excluding those which destroy or permanently damage the systems that are involved in them.

Coronary heart disease is probably the most serious stress-linked disease – in 1973 (in the UK) it accounted for 52% of all deaths of men between 45 and 54 years old and 41% of those between 24 and 44 years old (Joint Working Party, 1976) – a growing medical and public effort is being directed at reducing this increasing toll.

If an individual is affected, there must be repercussions for his or her family. Manager's wives, interviewed about moving, said of their husbands: 'If he's happy, we're happy' (Marshall and Cooper, 1976). Conversely, if one family member (especially one so 'powerful' as the head of the household) is showing symptoms of stress, this can seriously disrupt the whole pattern of family relationships. Seidenberg (1973) suggests that the stress thus caused helps to explain the recent rise, from 1:5 in 1962 to 1:2 in 1973, in the ratio of female to male alcoholics in the United States. A recent British study also depicts the wife as an indirect sufferer of stress effects – it concludes that the neglected wives of 'workaholic' executive husbands turn for compensation to involvement in the unsatisfactory middle-class housing estates in which they find themselves (*The Times*, 1975).

For the country's employers of manpower stress also has its costs, absenteeism being one of the more obvious. Stress-related illnesses are second and third in the table of those reasons for short-term sickness absence which are on the increase in Britain (Office of Health Economics, 1971). Between 1954/5 and 1967/8 'nervousness, debility and headaches' accounted for an increase of 189% of days off for men and 122% for women; 'psychoneurosis and psychosis' of +153% for men and +302% for women. Still using 'time off work' as our unit of measurement, we find that stress costs the economy substantially more than industrial injury (Taylor, 1974) and more than strikes (Gillespie, 1974). There are other less evident costs of stress to the employer: high labour turnover rates, poor staff morale and employees who do not find their jobs satisfying, all increase an organisation's costs whilst reducing its efficiency.

At a more macro-level, American writers have tried to calculate the cost of stress to the national economy. They include in their accounts such items as loss of production, treatment, prevention and the damage done by illegal behaviour. Their estimates (for the mid-1960s) are obviously no more than gross approximations; they range from an annual cost of six to twenty billion dollars (McMurray, 1973 and Conley *et al.*, 1973 respectively) or from 1% to 3% of the Gross National Product.

Having established stress as a topic of importance, it is appropriate to ask 'what are its causes?' and 'how can it be remedied?'. It is to the answer to these questions that this book is devoted. The primary objective of this volume therefore is to examine the subject of managerial stress in greater depth. Our intention is to do this in the following way. First, to provide a fuller understanding of the concept of stress, by focusing on its historical roots and underlying nature. Second, we will examine the research literature in the field of stress, as it might be appropriate for our understanding of the sources of managerial stress. This literature comes from a variety of social science and medical disciplines and these have been brought together here to give us a fuller perspective of the field. Third, to describe a major research effort (by the authors) to examine systematically the relationship between the health (both psychological and physical) of managers and the potential causes or sources of stress acting on them in their jobs and in their organisation. This is the first large-scale study of its kind which provides detailed data on this very important relationship. Fourth, to explore in-depth interview material obtained from a sample of the managers and their wives studied in the previous chapter. This helps us to go beyond the empirical data, to understand more fully the qualitative conflicts and dilemmas of stressful jobs. Fifth, we examine a number of issues, problems and contradictions that our assessment of managers under pressure raises, both conceptually and practically. We look at the kind of working model of stress our research has generated, at the relationship between job stress and job satisfaction, at the work:home interface as reflected by the changing role of managers' wives and at the methodological issues raised by this kind of research. Sixth, and finally, we discuss the remedies and prevention strategies that are open to us to minimise or alleviate stress.

2 Understanding the Nature and History of Stress as a Concept in the Social Sciences

'STRESS': A BRIEF HISTORY OF THE TERM

'Stress' (a word derived from Latin) was used popularly in the seventeenth century to mean 'hardship, straits, adversity or affliction' (Shorter Oxford English Dictionary, 1933). Only during the eighteenth and nineteenth centuries did its use evolve to denote 'force, pressure, strain or strong effort', with reference now also to objects, but still primarily to a person or a person's 'organs or mental powers' (Hinkle, 1973). It was these connotations, of an external pressure being resisted by the person/object which it sought to distort and disrupt, which were taken up when the term gained currency in engineering and physics. Although the concept was apparently employed by Boyle (investigating the properties of gases) and Hooke (elasticity of springs) in the seventeenth century, Hinkle (1973) credits its earliest precise definition to Baron Cauchy (Love, 1944) in the early nineteenth century. In physics then 'stress' refers to the internal force generated within a solid body by the action of any external force which tends to distort the body; 'strain' is the resulting distortion and the external force producing the distortion is called 'load'.

The idea that 'stress and strain' contribute to long-term ill-health (rather than merely short-term discomfort implicit in the above definition) can also be found early on in the concept's development. In 1910 for example Sir William Osler noted that *angina pectoris* was especially common among the Jewish members of the business community and attributed this, in part, to their hectic pace of life: 'Living an intense life, absorbed in his work, devoted to his pleasures, passionately devoted to his home, the nervous energy of the Jew is taxed to the uttermost, and his system is subjected to that stress and strain which seems to be a basic factor in so many cases of *angina pectoris*' (Osler, 1910).

The idea of distortion and the object's 'natural' (homeostatic or 'systemic equilibration') tendency to resist this is seen in Walter Cannon's use of the word stress in connection with his laboratory experiments on the 'fight or flight' reaction. He described his subjects (humans and animals) as being 'under stress', on observing reactions of the adrenal medulla and the sympathetic nervous system in the situations of cold, lack of oxygen, 'excitement', etc. to which he exposed them (Cannon, 1935).

That these same endocrine reactions could be elicited by a wide variety of damaging or alarming stimuli prompted Hans Selye to postulate a 'general adaptation syndrome' of somatic systems produced by 'non-specific stress' (Selye, 1946). Selye postulated three stages in the GAS:

1. the *alarm reaction* in which an initial shock phase of lowered resistance is followed by countershock during which the individual's defence mechanisms become active,
2. *resistance* – the stage of maximum adaptation and, hopefully, successful return to equilibrium for the individual. If however the stressor continues or defence does not work, he will move on to,
3. *exhaustion*, when adaptive mechanisms collapse.

This framework brings out a distinction between short- and long-term implications of harm already touched on above and suggests that ultimate outcomes even of stress can be beneficial. In current usage the immediate discomfort and anxiety (stage 1) are typically referred to as the 'stress reaction', whilst long-term sufferings (stage 3) are viewed as consequences of stress.

Although Selye's perspective is basically that of a medical doctor his contribution has had profound effects in many disciplines. His suggestion of non-specificity in reactions in particular has been widely accepted. (Hinkle, 1973 does question this idea claiming that 'the unique and essential characteristic of the response of the living organism to its environment is not its lack of specificity, but its high degree of specificity'. His criticism however is more an artefact of measurement – he is looking at verbal and behavioural reaction patterns, whereas Selye focused on raw physiological elements – than a true challenge.)

Also at work in the 1940s and 50s was Harold G. Wolff who contributed greatly to the application of the stress concept in general life situations rather than the confined stimulus-response laboratory setting. Many of the sources of Wolff's thinking are only now being 'rediscovered' by social scientists. He postulates a continuum of noxious stimuli from, at the one end those with 'unconditional' and direct action to, at the other end, those with more insidious influence:

Stimuli in the second category may be referred to as conditional and may be said to act indirectly. They may be of themselves biologically inconsequential or of extreme low intensity, and assume significance mainly because of their capacity to act as signals or symbols. They usually have little or no direct noxious effect. The nature of the adaptive reaction they evoke is dependent entirely upon individual past experience and to some degree upon the stock. They are less predictable and less stable, readily modified by the setting in which stimulation occurs, and there is commonly no close relationship in time between the stimulus and the response. Behavioural, attitudinal, and other bodily responses are only to a very limited degree appropriate in kind, as well as inappropriate in amount. They may, however, be long sustained and extremely destructive. These complex reactions during stress always involved the central nervous system, and especially the highest integrative function of the central nervous system. The meaning of the stimuli for the individual makes them assume the nature of stress (Wolff, 1953).

In this Wolff presages current day preoccupations with the vital role of interpretation.

Wolff sees stress as a state of the human organism and goes on to suggest that it is also an inevitable state of the human condition: 'Since stress is a dynamic state within an organism in response to a demand for adaptation, and since life itself entails constant adaptation, living creatures are continually in a state of more or less stress' (Wolff, 1968).

In Wolff's thinking we see many of the vital elements which have helped to progress the concept of stress from the 'mechanical' model of the previous generation to today's interpretative psychological orientation. He was however somewhat before his time and must be ignored here if the mainstream of conceptualisation is to be followed. Figure 2.1 is a summary of the stimulus-response approach:

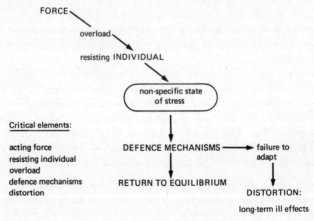

FIGURE 2.1 The hypothesised stress reaction up to the 1950s

'STRESS': CURRENT USAGE

Many current definitions of stress stick fairly closely to the homeostatic, energy-exchange models of Cannon and the other early researchers.

Caplan (1964) adopting a simple stimulus-response approach depicts man as reacting to situations with learned coping mechanisms activated by homeostatic principles and fuelled by energies which are in finite supply. Problems arise when the organism's supplies are insufficient to meet the physical, psychological and/or sociocultural demands made of them.

Cofer and Appley (1964) offer a similar definition: 'Stress is the state of an organism where he perceives that his well-being (or integrity) is endangered and that he must divert all his energies to its protection.'

Basowitz, Persky, Korchin and Grinker (1955) also bring out implications of overload: 'We should not consider stress as imposed upon the organism, but as its response to internal or external processes which reach those threshold levels that strain its physical and psychological integrative capacities close to or beyond their limits.' At the same time they mention the response the individual makes as a necessary component of stress definition. This more sophisticated viewpoint is particularly well articulated by Lazarus. Whilst pointing out that both the environmental stimulus and the reacting individual are vital elements (one cannot refer to a stimulus as such unless it is part of a reactive situation, etc.), he emphasises that it is the nature of the relationship between the two which is crucial: 'Stress refers then to a very broad class of problems differentiated from other problem areas because it deals with *any demands which tax the system*, whatever it is, a physiological system, a social system, or a psychological system, *and the response of that system*' (Lazarus, 1971). He goes on to say that the 'reaction depends on how the person interprets or appraises (consciously or unconsciously) the significance of a harmful, threatening or challenging event.'

'Cognitive appraisal' is an essentially individual-based affair: 'The appraisal of threat is not a simple perception of the elements of the situation, but a judgement, an inference in which the data are assembled to a constellation of ideas and expectations' (Lazarus, 1966). Change in any one element – e.g. the background situation against which the stimulus is perceived – can radically alter the perceiver's interpretation.

Appley (1962) agrees that this cognitive element (he calls it 'threat perception') is the vital link between the individual's environment and his experience of stress. Arnold (1960) prefers the term 'sense judgement' and emphasises that elaborate levels of awareness are not necessarily involved.

Once this 'perceptual viewpoint' becomes theoretically acceptable we find that researchers soon seek to ascribe some of the (indisputable) individual variations in nature and levels of stress to characteristics of the individual rather than, as before, concentrating mainly on the environment. Appley and Trumbull (1967) talk of a person's 'vulnerability profile' – personality, demographic factors, physical make-up, past experience and motivation will be the main considerations here – and quote substantiating research which found that 'well-adjusted, integrated, mature' individuals showed less performance decrement in stress situations than did persons not so classified. They add that the more the stimulus relies on prior conditioning, the more individual differences are likely to play a part.

A term which we must clarify before proceeding is 'load', i.e. the environmental demand experienced by the individual. As we have seen most writers focus on overload of the organisms capabilities as causing stress; engineering's use of the word encourages this interpretation. We now have however experimental evidence (e.g. studies of sensory isolation, stimulus impoverishment and social isolation) to show that underload too is 'unacceptable'. Kahn (1970) points to the implication from engineering that conditions of zero stress favour maximum life for the structure concerned and suggests that it is totally invalid to apply this to living organisms. Weick (1970) developing this idea (and in doing so agreeing with Wolff's concept of stress as a natural condition of man) feels that 'a more realistic view is that a person experiences more or less stress, not presence or absence of stress.'

Drawing together the preceding two points we see that, rather than being either response- or situation-based, the concept of stress truly makes sense only when seen as imbalance in the context of an organism–environment transaction. Most writers endorse this person–environment fit model in their discussions if not their definitions of stress. It is summarised in Figure 2.2.

One dissenter from the ranks who is perhaps worthy of note here is Hinkle (1973). He fundamentally questions the continuing need for the concept of a state of stress as an intervening variable between systems now known to have direct relationships:

> The 'stress' explanation is no longer necessary. It is evident that any disease process, and in fact any process within the living organism, might be influenced by the reaction of the individual to his social environment or to other people. . . . These mechanisms are either understood or potentially understandable on a straightforward physiological basis. It is not necessary to invoke a special variable called 'stress' in order to understand their occurrence.

Hinkle's further contention that: 'It is hard to conceive of a "state of stress" within an organism which is qualitatively different from any other state of being alive' adds to his scepticism as to the need for the concept of 'stress'. His theme has merit but as yet appears to have had little impact on researchers in this area.

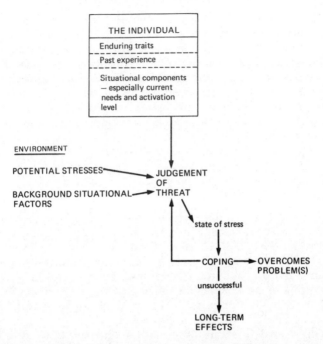

FIGURE 2.2 The stress reaction: current consensus, a question of person: environment fit

Throughout the above presentation we have stuck doggedly to using 'stress' to denote a state of the organism as this is consistent with the theoretical development outlined and because other more general uses of the term – e.g. a 'stressful event' – imply that this state is a matter of 'fact'. Sadly however rigour in theoretical definition and practical usage do not always concur. Few writers use the word consistently and 'stress' is used to denote variously:

1. an excessive environmental force (e.g. too much work) which, by its actions on an individual, causes him harm
2. the harm thus caused (fatigue)
3. the individual's reactions in such a situation (irritability, inability to concentrate).

It has been applied to small groups, organisations and societies as well as individual people and physical structures (e.g. bridges). Its manifestations have been looked for at physiological, psychological, psycho-social and behavioural levels and it has been linked (usually without prior justification) to anxiety, dissatisfaction, self-esteem and many other supposedly more easily measurable states.

Variations in the meaning ascribed to 'stress' are frequently due to differences in researchers' academic backgrounds and/or data-gathering approaches. Within disciplines they are also a reflection of confusion/argument as to which of the elements are the independent and dependent variables in the particular experiment or survey being considered. These confusions all pose problems when one is trying to compare results or integrate findings. In reviewing the more practically biased literature that follows an appreciation of variations in semantics is vital and this will be given wherever both appropriate and possible.

CONSEQUENCES AND MANIFESTATIONS OF STRESS

The implication that the effects of stress are somehow 'undesirable' has been made several times above. Whilst it is accepted by researchers that 'stress' can have both short- and long-term adverse effects on an individual's mental and physical health, there is much debate as to the nature, and probabilities, of the causal relationships involved. We do not propose to become too entangled in the complexities of this (highly 'technical') material here, but shall briefly summarise current thinking about the consequences of stress.

The mental ill-effects of stress (e.g. anxiety, lowered self-esteem, depression) are intuitively credible and are frequently used as measures of stress. Rather than being 'effects by proof' they are very much 'effects by definition'. Over the last 10 to 15 years stress has also been linked with various physical symptoms such as high blood pressure and blood cholesterol levels, rashes and alopecia. These are physical signs of high activation levels and thus are also symptoms that the individual is 'in a state of stress'. Over time these physical symptoms can have their own undesirable consequences; most notably coronary heart disease but also peptic ulcers, rheumatoid arthritis and diabetes (Hanse, 1974). This is how Hinkle (1973) summarises the evidence on this topic:

> In other words, it might be said that, in man and in the higher animals, reactions to the environment which are mediated by the sense organs and the central nervous system have the capacity to influence any process within the organism that can be influenced by the gross motor behaviour of the organism itself, or by the alteration of any function of either the organism or of its component parts, which can be influenced by the skeletal or autonomic nervous system, or by the glands of internal secretion, acting alone or together. . . . Thus the potential magnitude of the effects . . . appears to be as great as the effects which can be produced by any other influences upon these processes, not even excluding those which destroy or permanently damage the systems that are involved in them.

Whilst the general paradigm is constantly being supported by new evidence the progression from stress experience to coronary heart disease is by no means a hundred per cent certainty. Many other variables – such as personality, life style, social support, occupation, diet and cigarette smoking – have been identified as influencing the interactions involved. At a recent conference for air traffic controllers, Carruthers (1976) mapped the probable contributions of some of these:

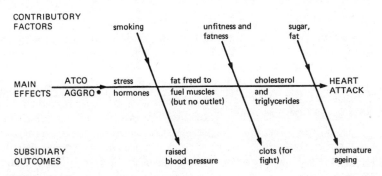

FIGURE 2.3 Flight path to a heart attack
* ATCO AGGRO – refers to Air Traffic Control Officer aggravation.

Underlying many writers' descriptions of this fatal sequence of effects is the belief that man reacts physically in threat situations where physical discharge is no longer appropriate. The resulting 'bottling up' only feeds his inner tension and over time has irreversible physiological consequences. The implications too that 'stress' is the Black Plague of the twentieth century cannot be ignored.

Stress is acknowledged as a study topic of vital importance not only because of the mental and physical suffering it can cause individuals but also because it may well make a substantial, if indirect, contribution to the social and economic problems of today's society. Many writers justify their interest in stress as a research topic by its cost to the national economy (Felton and Cole, 1963; Aldridge, 1970; Gillespie, 1974; Taylor 1974). Whilst the figures will not be quoted here it is obvious that the economic cost of stress in terms of absenteeism, sick leave pay and hospital bills is considerable.

EARLY RECOGNITION OF STRESS SYMPTOMS

In a restricted context several writers (mostly company doctor types) have identified symptoms of managerial stress which can be recognised in behaviour at work (Kenton, 1974; Pettigrew, 1972; McGhee, 1963; Webber 1966). Consistently mentioned are:

1. difficulty in thinking rationally and seeing all the problem
2. rigidity of views, prejudice
3. out-of-place aggression and irritability
4. withdrawal from relationships
5. excessive smoking
6. an inability to relax resulting in excessive drinking or a need for sleeping pills.

To conclude, whilst the complexity and conditional nature of inter-actions between the individual and his environment make nonsense of any attempt to summarise life in a few simple, causal, one-to-one relationships there is wide agreement, especially amongst the medical profession, that there is a strong link between experience of stress and 'premature' death.

THREE DATA-GATHERING APPROACHES ADOPTED IN 'THE STRESS FIELD'

The situations studied as bases for the definitions and theories of stress considered above can be classified into three basic types: experimental, trauma situations and general life. In this section we shall illustrate the first two only briefly and then go on to deal more extensively with literature generated by the third, which is the perspective adopted in the study described in this book. (For extensive treatment of conceptual and methodological issues in the experimental and 'trauma' areas see Appley and Trumbull, 1967 and McGrath, 1970).

EXPERIMENTAL STUDIES

In experimental, usually laboratory, studies of stress the subject (often an animal) is presented with stimuli predefined by the experimenter as stress-inducing; its reactions are then monitored. The emphasis is at the stimulus-response level of analysis of controllable, discrete, observable behaviours. Often gross assumptions about the meaning of the experience for the individual are made. For example whilst all the evidence suggests that physiologically 'positive emotions', such as excitement or pleasure, are indistinguishable from 'negative emotions' (fear, anxiety or anger) elevated activation levels are frequently used in-discriminately as 'indices of stress'. Other highly defined (and assump-tive) measures of stress found in this type of work are performance on learning tasks and normality of response on word association or projective personality tests. (See for example Hackman, 1970 for a detailed discussion of 'experimental tasks'.)

These researchers are open to criticism because they study behaviours in isolation. Corson (1970) for example warns against previous researchers in his field (animal studies) who have 'focused their attention on, and drawn conclusions from, the measurement of a few isolated variables *without due regard to the place of these variables in the total integrative adaptive activity of the organism.*'

Interpretation and extrapolation are also major problems. Corson himself goes on to cite studies of the reactions of dogs unable to avoid receiving electric shocks to suggest that unavoidable stresses and insoluble problems cause anxiety in man. Whilst we would intuitively agree with his suggestion, it is only tenuously substantiated by his research results. Ethical considerations usually dictate that any discomfort that is imposed upon the subject should be short-lived (especially with human subjects); it is also difficult therefore to be more than speculative about long-term consequences.

An ambitious extension of the experimental approach is seen in a study of sports parachutists who were asked to indicate their anxiety level on a 10-point scale at 14 different time points during a parachute jump (Epstein and Fenz, 1965). Whilst the results of this and similar experiments have prompted extremely interesting speculation on such topics as anticipatory fear, denial, generalisation, indiscriminate sensitisation and the function of preparatory information, the practical problems of taking this controlled approach 'out into the field' are obvious.

TRAUMA SITUATIONS

A second group of researchers, whilst still dealing with phenomena which occur at a particular point in time, have studied real-life problems of trauma, crisis and extreme situations. Here stress is seldom measured as such; it is assumed to be present as an integral component of 'what is happening'. Two main disciplines have contributed to this field – the medical psychologists with their studies of illness, dying and bereavement, combat, space travel, being a prisoner of war or refugee, etc. and the sociologists who discuss 'ordinary' life transitions (such as going to college or marriage) in terms of identity crises. Both groups speak, sometimes with surprise, of the potential positive outcomes of these interludes although the implication is that usually the experience is traumatic at the time.

The notion of 'stages' is common to both approaches. Bowlby (1960) for example, discussing young children and the grief of separation, describes three phases – protest, despair and detachment. His paradigm is however atypical as it does not end with a return to 'normal'. Janis

(1969) talks of progression through the stages of mourning as a necessary part of healing for the bereaved and suggests, from his studies of
anticipatory fear in surgical patients, that there is danger in 'failure to
carry out the work of worrying'. In more active 'emergency situations'
Glass (1970) postulates 'pre-impact', 'warning', 'recoil' and 'post-
impact' phases. Fink (Fink, Beak and Taddeo, 1971) also maps out stages
in reaction to crisis (shock → defensive retreat → acknowledge-
ment → adaptation and change) and applies his model in detail and
quite convincingly not only to the individual but also to an organisation and its functioning.

The sociological literature, particularly, assumes the potential for
beneficial outcomes in the crises it studies. The implication is for example
the basic tenet of Erikson's theory of personality development which
he depicts as a progression through eight identity formation 'battles'
(from that between Trust and Mistrust during infancy to Integrity versus
Disgust and Despair in mature life) each of which must be 'won' if a
healthy adult is to emerge (Erikson, 1959). Glaser and Strauss (1969)
adopt a similar approach to a wide class of events which they term
'status passages' (any changes in role). Parkes (1971) and Rapoport and
Rapoport (1964) prefer the term 'critical role transitions' in their discussions of maturational changes such as engagement and marriage.

That 'crises' can even be beneficial at the time is suggested by reports
of improved health and morale during disruption – for example of
refugees when fleeing from Hungary in 1956 (Hinkle, 1974).

The literature in this section is preoccupied with outcomes and
therefore pays much attention to reactions and coping. Denial appears
to be a particularly effective, and many claim necessary, defence
mechanism in the early stages of trauma. Hinkle (1974) for example
describes Chinese immigrants in New York who were unaffected despite
such a major culture shock experience as being 'insulated'. Later on information and social support become important. The former acts as a
weapon against uncertainty and anxiety whilst the latter provides a safe
background against which reconstruction of disintegrated systems can
be experimented with and achieved.

The agreement is that, whatever coping does take place, time is
required for it to be accomplished but within this generalisation few
quantified findings are available. McGrath (1970) suggests that 'time
may be one of the most important and most neglected, parameters of
the problem.' As part of an extensive debate (some of which will appear
below in 'Theoretical Issues') he cites the failure of warnings that
cigarette smoking leads to cancer to affect many peoples' behaviour, to
suggest that, if too long is allowed for coping, the situation loses its
potency and the stimulus is ignored.

From this section we learn several things which are of relevance in a
managerial setting – but especially that disruption and temporary dis-

comfort are inevitable and necessary components of life's natural role changes and are beneficial (even pleasurable) in both wider and long-term contexts.

GENERAL LIFE

The third 'approach to stress' is that which looks at facets of the individual (some would claim to study the whole) in his day-to-day interactions with the environment. Research in this field covers a wide range of 'focus' variables – here we shall deal only with those of particular relevance to this book and shall in places pre-empt the section on managerial stress to point out this relevance.

(i) *Community studies*

Some of the most general of these studies have been community studies of which the major examples are from the United States (Orole *et al.*, 1962; Leighton *et al.*, 1963; Gurin *et al.*, 1960). The main outcome has been a concern that the incidence of mental ill-health (the typical criterion of 'stress') is so high, especially since it is usually well above that predicted from health-care agency statistics of known patients. Research results are usually complicated and either difficult to interpret or intuitively obvious. They will not therefore be reported here.

The methodological problems of these studies have been considerable-rigour in the classification of psychiatric health is usually a major drain on research effort but remains open to debate. Correlation of variables cannot be taken as proof of causality or direction of effect (Dohrenwend, 1961, cites 'the well-known drift hypothesis' to illustrate how poor mental health could effect the social order rather than the other way round) and the confounding interrelationships of many variables (e.g. age and physical health) make simplified interpretations impossible. Preservation of the complexity is however feasible and Indik, Seashore and Slesinger (1964) refer to the patterns in Gurin's (1960) data as keys to the 'stress values of different social roles'. This idea is echoed in the brief treatment of occupational differences below.

(ii) *Change*

Research work that points to the fact that rapid change (an intrinsic element of civilised society today) is a source of stress to the population at large (Toffler, 1970; Taylor, 1972) and the urban segment in particular is also at a fairly general level. Bornstein and Bornstein (1976) give results of an international study to show 'that pace of life (measured here by walking velocity) varies in a regular fashion with the size of the local population regardless of the cultural setting'. Carlestan (1971) offers figures which suggest that those in big cities (in Sweden) are under greater 'strain' (his measures are incidence of lung cancer and the percentage of 'habitual' drinkers) than those in other urban areas who in turn are more at risk than those who live in rural areas.

Managers, by being more likely to live and/or work in urban areas, to travel and to be constantly doing new and varied things, are subjected to more risk on this general change dimension than many other occupational groups.

(iii) *Life changes*

Researchers have tried to measure change effects by focusing on actual events in an individual's life. A considerable body of work along these lines in the last fifteen years has led to the suggestion that life change *per se* is a pre-conditioning factor to illness.

Wyler, Holmes and Masuda, a group of research workers at Washington University, conducted a survey (Wyler, Masuda and Holmes, 1971, Holmes and Masuda, 1973) from which they calculated the relative amounts of 'social adjustment' required after certain life events. They were then able to apply these weightings to the events in the lives of selected sample populations and to arrive at their 'life change scores' for a given period. In their studies (which have been both retrospective and prospective) they have found high life change scores to be related to the onset of illness within the following two-year period. Correlational studies suggest a relationship between life change score and the onset of tuberculosis, heart disease, skin disease and hernia, a general deterioration in health and poorer academic performance (Holmes and Masuda, 1973). Wyler, Masuda and Holmes (1971) also purport to show that the greater the life change experienced the more serious the disease that develops. Myers, Lindenthal and Pepper (1971) also found a relationship between life events and psychiatric symptomatology in a community study in Connecticut. A net increase in life events was associated with worsening symptoms, a net decrease with improvement. These researchers contend that the nature of the change – whether it is favourable or unfavourable, competitive or complementary – is immaterial.

The global applicability of these findings has however been challenged, particularly on methodological issues. Brown, Sklair, Harris and Birley (1973) and Mechanic (1974) provide extensive reviews of the many research problems. Acting on some of these criticisms they and other researchers have made considerable refinements to the original techniques and have gone on to establish relationships between certain classes of life events and, for example, alcoholic relapse or the onset of schizophrenia. While the simplistic nature of Holmes *et al*'s early findings is now being questioned, their basic conclusion that there is a link between change in life events and the onset of illness is generally accepted.

Managers, particularly those headed for top positions, show high life change scores on measures of the Holmes and Rahe type. In work subsidiary to this study it was attempted to relate life change scores to health (measured on the Gurin scale to be described later) and global life satisfaction for two populations of managers – ones who were being relocated versus those who were 'stationary' (Marshall and Cooper, 1976). The movers had significantly elevated change scores not only for the time at which they were studied but also for the preceding two years – a reflection of the demanding and 'changeful' natures of their jobs at that particular point in their careers. For the non-movers life change scores were significantly related to health in the expected direction (at $p > 0.025$) but showed no consistent relationship with expressed satisfaction. For the movers ($n = 15$) high change scores were correlated with better physical health ($p > 0.10$) but lower satisfaction ($p > 0.025$). Despite the small samples involved, these results are consistent with those of a dissenting band of other researchers in suggesting that the nature of the change involved may be relevant and that effects may vary across life areas.

(iv) *Mobility and status incongruence*

Mobility is a special case of change. Mobility studies have concentrated on examining trends in four basic demographic variables – ethnic group, educational level, occupation and geographic location. Mobility refers to any upward or downward trend in these and is sometimes measured using the subject's parents as a standard (e.g. a senior manager whose father is a bricklayer would be classified as upwardly mobile). Whilst some studies have examined relationships between single dimensions and the dependent variables (of which high blood pressure and job dissatisfaction are common examples) others have tried to incorporate several or all variables as a global measure of 'cultural mobility'.

Mobility is just one of a multitude of factors which has been included in retrospective and prospective studies aimed at discriminating the precursors of cardiovascular heart disease and its related risk factors (high blood pressure, serum cholesterol levels, etc.). Overall these studies support the hypotheses that risk of heart disease rises with job level and decreases with the amount of physical activity involved in the job. (For a comprehensive survey of this data see Smith (1967).) Some studies also report higher risks with greater geographic mobility – Syme, Hyman and Enterline (1965) report a higher incidence of heart disease onset for the occupationally mobile (four or more job changes) and the geographically mobile (two or more 'cross-country' moves) than for stable comparison groups. In a more complex multivariant analysis of self-reported coronary cases Syme, Borhani and Beuchley (1965) found that high mobility (an index combining ethnic, occupational and geographical data) was related to disease incidence independently of other major risk factors such as cigarette smoking, weight and job activity levels. The relationship however is not well supported. Hinkle (1973) for example reports a carefully controlled long-term study of 1152 employees of the Bell Telephone Company during which he found no significant relationships between his nine measures of organisational mobility (number of promotions, time since last promotion, departmental transfer, etc.) and death from or onset of coronary heart disease or death from other causes.

A much more widely applicable explanation of the data is provided by the concept of 'status inconsistency' and the social discontinuities it leads to. Shekelle, Ostfeld and Paul (1969) for example in a prospective study of a medically examined industrial population discovered that men were at a significantly higher risk of CHD when their social class in childhood, or the wife's social class in her childhood, was higher or lower than the class level that they presently shared. Kasl and Cobb (1967) also found that parental status stress appears to be a variable having strong, long-term effects on physical and mental health of adult offspring. Daughters of mothers whose educational level was inappropriate to the latter's husband's occupational level for example showed statistically significantly higher incidences of rheumatoid arthritis and self-reported anger than those whose parents were judged 'congruent'.

Berry (1966) found among a 6131 national sample that a small amount of variance in morbidity rate (incidence of hospitalisation) was explained by status inconsistency. In more specific relation to occupations the consistency of occupational level with other status considerations (e.g., education, race) has been identified as a source of stress. Jackson (1962) for example reports that members of his sample whose ethnic race was superior to their occupational rank showed a high level of stress symptoms. Christenson and Hinkle (1961) found that high school graduates filling managerial jobs showed more symptoms considered prognostic of later CHD (elevated systolic and diastolic blood pressures, overweight, etc.) than did colleagues at the same level who had had the benefit of college education.

A complementary research approach and one which is of particular relevance here has been to look at the occupational status an individual actually achieves compared with that which he 'deserves' (or feels he deserves). Brook (1973) provided four very interesting case studies of individuals showing behavioural disorders as a result of being either over-promoted (when a person has reached the peak of his abilities with little possibility of further development and is given responsibility exceeding his capacity) or under-promoted (not given responsibility commensurate with ability level). In each case the progression of the status disorder was from minor psychological symptoms (e.g. palpitations, episodes of panic, etc.) to marked psychosomatic complaints and then to mental illness.

Erikson and Gunderson of the US Navy Neuropsychiatric Unit are developing a comprehensive research programme in the US Navy to assess systematically this problem which they term 'status congruence' or the matching of one individual's advancement with his experience and ability. In an earlier study Arthur and Gunderson (1965) found that promotional lag was significantly related to psychiatric illness. Later Erikson, Pugh and Gunderson (1972) found that Navy personnel experienced greater job satisfaction when their rates of advancement exceeded (although not excessively) their expectation; dissatisfaction increased as advancement rates were retarded. Those who were least successful with regard to advancement tended to perceive the greatest amount of stress in their lives. In a more recent study by Erikson, Edwards and Gunderson (1973) it was found among a sample of over 9000 Navy ratings that (1) status congruency was negatively related to the incidence of psychiatric disorder and (2) that status congruency was positively related to military effectiveness.

Whilst the results on 'status incongruence' present fairly consistent findings it is dangerous to overgeneralise in this field where most researchers are using grossly simplified variables. 'Incongruence' may for instance not always be an easy dimension to measure. From a study in which he interviewed the 20 telephone operators who had had least illness and the 20 who had had most illness over the preceding 20 years (out of a source population of 336), Hinkle (1974) concluded that the main difference between the two groups was that the 'interests' of the former coincided with their 'circumstances' whereas the latter were not so fortunate. Jackson (1962) reached a more differentiated conclusion about status incongruence 'that all forms of status inconsistency are psychologically disturbing, but response to stress varies with relative positions of inconsistent person's achieved and ascribed status ranks'.

What evidence is there to suggest that managers are subject to these particular strains? As regards geographic mobility they are probably the most mobile sector of British society today and the fact that younger segments of the managerial population are moving more than others suggests that this is an accelerating trend (House, 1969). Pahl and Pahl (1971), in a fairly small sample of 'middle-class managers', found that 22% had moved workplace once every two or three years and a further 33% once every four or five years. There was a tendency for commercial functions to be more mobile than the technical ones. Birch and Macmillan (1970) in a study of 2000 British Institute of Management members found wide variations in movement patterns. On average their (not necessarily representative) sample had changed employers 2.7 times per career and changed job within a company 2.9 times per career. It should be noted that there were wide variations within their sample: substantial numbers had experienced no movement (17% for company and 17% for job within company) and others were highly mobile (19% and 24% respectively had changed five times or more).

Several factors contribute to these high mobility levels. One is an organisational attitude, now possibly undergoing a 'rethink', that employees, like components, are transferable units of production and should be utilised as such to achieve a flexible work force (25% of the moves reported in a British study by House (1969) were compulsory, 'within' company relocations). Managers have contributed to the development of the moving ethic (particularly in the United States where there is more concern than in the UK) by failing to resist. Some fear that they might lose their jobs if they do so, but a more powerful, and ominous, explanation is that mobility has come to be an inherent part of career development – 'travel is the hallmark of success' as Seidenberg (1973) puts it.

Writers agree that the monetary advantages of moving are small, if they exist at all. Roche (1975) claims that, rather than money, managers are seeking 'self-actualisation'. Immundo (1974) talks of the high task and achievement orientation of managers for whom movement becomes an end in itself. Jennings (1967) puts the case even more strongly: 'The manager who centres his life style upon mobility is the conformist' and advocates that both he and his family learn to like this state of affairs. Further substantiating evidence comes from the complementary claim by Morris (1956) that research has shown more psychosomatic illness from being 'passed over' than from achieving high management positions.

It is doubtful whether this trend towards mobility can continue indefinitely. Managers have become more demanding and the result is that movement is an increasing cost to the company; there is also, it is said, a growing concern for family life and how it might be affected. In America Seidenberg (1973) asks if the early 'moving mania' is being checked. He states that in 1971 66% of executives expected to be moved every three years and that in 1973 only 37% were in that situation. Improved communications have helped to make this reversal possible.

Social mobility is also likely to be high amongst executives. Management levels are likely to include a substantial number of those who are moving upward. Selection is largely qualification-based and university education is now available for all. As it would appear however that one cannot experience university life or the life style of a manager without in many ways 'becoming' middle-class (e.g. Braine, 1962; Nichols, 1971) –

status incongruence may well be a pressure on those from lower social classes.

(v) *Occupation and occupational differences*

There is a growing body of research evidence to suggest that work is a major source of stress – this is hardly surprising in view of the dominant role that it plays in most people's lives. The literature dealing with the occupational group selected for study here – managers – will be reviewed in a section of its own below. In portraying managers as a group 'at risk' in society, we are not making a claim that they suffer more 'stress' than other occupational groups. It is more realistic to view different sectors of society in terms of the distinctive pattern of pressures that they face. Paced-assembly line workers for example might suffer from monotonous work in poor physical conditions with no let-up; policemen in this country are complaining of overload, too much paperwork and social isolation from the rest of the community (*The Guardian*, 1974); the problems of managers will be a different, probably unique, configuration of work demands and employee motivations.

Substantiating evidence for this viewpoint comes from an extensive American study of job stresses across 23 occupational groups, pre-selected as being potentially high-stress (Caplan *et al.*, 1975). Total sample size was 2010 and the other variables measured were: strain ('any deviation from normal responses in the person'), health-related behaviours, personality, subjective environment (workload, responsibility for people and things, etc.) and 'person-environment fit' on six dimensions. Whilst the results are highly complex and only univariate analysis is so far available, two clusters of stressful job characteristics appear to be emerging:

(i) low utilisation of abilities, low participation, low work complexity and poor person–environment fit – exemplified by assembly line workers.

(ii) high quantitative workload, a need for sustained concentration, and high responsibility for people – these were typical of administrative professors and physicians who also scored highest on a measure of the coronary-prone personality.

(vi) *Occupational level and inactivity*

At a more global level there are a number of studies which relate the two main stress measures, cardiovascular heart disease and mental ill-health (CHD and MIH), to occupational level of which Marks (1967) provides an excellent review. The majority of these studies support the proposition that risk of CHD rises with occupational level (Ryle and Russell, 1949; Breslow and Buell, 1960; McDonough, *et al.,* 1965; Syme, Hyman and Enterline, 1964: Wardwell, Hyman and Bahnson, 1964). Substantial national analyses of both British and American mortality data lend support to these studies. Not all researchers however are in agreement. Pell and D'Alonzo (1958) in a highly self-consistent longitudinal study of Dupont employees found that incidence of myocardial infarction was inversley related to salary roll level. Stamler, Kjelisberg and Hall (1960) and Bainton and Peterson (1963) also came up with contradictory results. A further group of researchers have added confusion by finding no relationship between CHD and occupation; Berkson (1960) for blue-versus white-collar Negroes, Spain (1969) for Jewish salesmen versus other occupational groupings and Paul (1963) for different job levels at the Western Electric Company. The gross nature of classifications used in these studies has contributed to the confusion of results, particularly as some researchers have concentrated on occupational levels and others on discrete occupational groupings. The trend now is to look in more detail at significant job components, in order to explain differential CHD rates. Several studies for example have tried to assess whether in-activity or increased intellectual and emotional job demands contribute most to the increased risk of CHD with occupational level. Whilst the high positive correlation of these two in actual job situations makes this debate somewhat 'academic' it would appear likely that the latter is of greater importance. Intuitively the physical activity of a clerk is not likely to be substantially less than that of a managing director yet his risk of developing CHD is not so high. Two studies quoted by Marks also come to this conclusion: in the first, farm owners were found to be more susceptible to CHD than farm labourers despite comparable activity rates (McDonough *et al.,* 1965); and in the second, 'downturn' bus drivers (sedentary) and conductors (active) had higher CHD than their suburban counterparts (Morris, 1953).

(vii) *Novels and the popular press*

As stress plays such a large part in most people's lives, it is not surprising that it has provided a topic for non-academic writers. Fisher (1970), Heller (1975), and Wilson (1972) for example deal specifically with the work environment.

Stress is also becoming an increasingly 'trendy' topic in the popular press in this country (e.g. *Homes and Gardens,* 1974; *Times Colour Magazine,* 1976). The basic material is usually drawn either from academic research or case histories but is often poorly reported, if not completely distorted, by the typical eclectic journalist's needs for impact and readership.

The emergence of this literature is however of interest here for several reasons:

1. it means that certain sections of the public feel that stress is a real problem
2. as the debate enlarges hopefully there will be less social stigma attached to 'being under stress' which will make research in the area easier on several counts and may also reduce one source of stress, and
3. being aware of this literature will feed into the individual's experience of stress and his reporting of it.

GENERAL ISSUES ARISING

In this section, we shall briefly mention some of the subsidiary theoretical issues that should be borne in mind in this area. We shall raise questions (to most of which there are as yet no answers) as a way of illustrating: (i) how practically inadequate the above conceptualisations can be and (ii) the essential complexity of the topic.

QUESTION 1. IS STRESS (ALWAYS) BAD?

Physiologically 'stress' is similar to other, reportedly enjoyable, states of elevated activation (Froberg, Karlsson, Levi and Lidberg, 1971). (Bernard (1968) proposes that these should be differentiated linguistically, calling unpleasant stress 'dystress' and pleasant stress 'eustress'.) Stress situations are often the impetuses for adaptions and changes which are beneficial in the long term. Much of human behaviour can be construed as actively seeking stressful situations ('challenges'). As Corneille (1666) says; 'We triumph without glory when we conquer without danger'. The total elimination of stress could therefore greatly reduce the quality of life.

QUESTION 2. WHAT IS THE RELATIONSHIP BETWEEN PSYCHOLOGICAL AND PHYSIOLOGICAL SYMPTOMS OF STRESS?

The idea that primitive apeman is trapped in a civilised society which does not allow him to dissipate stress naturally (i.e. physically) suggests that the various response media are alternative rather than summative. Research tends to support this idea; McGrath (1970) reports that intercorrelations between psychological, physiological and behavioural indices are poor. For example in a public speaking exercise stutterers

reported only moderate emotion (psychological), but were 'clearly em-
barrassed' (behavioural) and showed adrenaline excretion rates up 150%
compared to the 40% of controls (physiological) (Leanderson and Levi,
1967). Lazarus (1967) also reports that experimental subjects who consistently used denial as a coping technique reported less anxiety than
non-deniers but showed bigger physiological reactions.

If these 'systems' are alternatives it is dangerous to add together the
various symptoms to achieve a cumulative measure of stress intensity as
so many researchers do.

QUESTION 3A. HOW DOES COPING CONTRIBUTE TO THE SITUATION?

The individual's coping response, just like his threat perception, is an
integral part of the situation: 'How a person experiences the
pathological process, what it means to him and how this meaning influences his behaviour and interaction with others are all integral components of disease viewed as a total human response' (Lipawski, 1969).

It could well add to the stress experienced: the desire to deal with a
threat inappropriately for instance might also prove stressful and set off
a spiral of effects. McGrath (1970b) feels that research like stress should
be cyclic: 'The legitimate business of stress research is the tracing out of
these *sequences* of events which take place between environment (embed-
ding system) and focal organism.'

Coping is not only reactive:

it can take place before and during 'the stress experience',
it can be anticipatory or preventative,
it can be directed at the environment or at the consequences,
one or several techniques can be employed, or if the individual uses
multiple techniques, these can be simultaneous or successive. (See
McGrath (1970a) for a fuller discussion.)

Steiner (1970) investigated some of these issues in a contrived
disagreement situation in which four coping responses were
admissable – conformity, rejection, devaluation of the issue and under-
recall of disagreement. Using skin conductance as a measure of 'tension', he found that subjects who consistently used a particular coping
method (no matter which) showed less tension than those who had no
preferred method; they also responded more slowly. Steiner's results
raise several issues: How stable would the preferred strategy be across
different situations? What would happen when it was inappropriate?
Was quick response an alternative (but unexpected) strategy for coping
with tension? Does use of one of these ('unsatisfactory') coping
techniques mean that no stress is perceived? Does it mean that there are
therefore no physiological ill-effects?

QUESTION 3B. HOW CAN WE JUDGE WHETHER A PARTICULAR INSTANCE OF COPING IS ADAPTIVE OR MALADAPTIVE?

Is this judgement to be made for the short- or long-term outcomes? With reference to what system should it be made? Which needs or goals of that system should be taken into account?

Dohrenwend (1961) talks of the 'adaptation to constraint' as having three facets – affective, conative and cognitive – and argues that a coping behaviour must be assessed against a base-line combination of these. Kahn (1970) emphasises the need to look at the outcomes for the larger system in which the 'focus individual' is embedded – for example coping that is maladaptive for a particular manager (e.g. working excessive hours) may well have benefits for the company. Altman and Lett (1970) put forward another reason for taking an ecological approach – that we may come to understand how the individual uses his environment to cope with stress.

QUESTION 4. ARE THERE DIFFERENT TYPES OF LOAD?

Above we have briefly mentioned the evidence that underload is also a source of stress (and shall return to this in a work context later). Here we might conceptually differentiate quantitative from qualitative load; acknowledge that differential load might act on different parts of the organism; wonder how the effects of various combinations of short- ('acute') and long-term ('chronic') load might differ and speculate that variations in the individual's response capabilities (tiredness, monotony, etc.) will influence the subjective load felt from the same objective stimulus.

QUESTION 5. WHAT ABOUT TIMING?

Several of the above 'issues' have pointed to a need to take a tighter hold on the time aspects of stress research. McGrath (1970a) feels that 'time may be one of the most important, and most neglected, parameters of the problem' and calls for time-oriented studies, both longitudinal and looking at micro-temporal factors.

An example of an experiment where time was the sole manipulated variable was that carried out by Brady (1966) as part of his 'executive' monkey research. He found that intermittent stress was more likely to create ulcers than was chronic stress and hypothesised that in the latter situation some type of stable adjustment occurred. Such evidence suggests that we do indeed need to pay greater attention to this factor.

In this chapter we have used the available literature to bring out what appear to be the relevant elements in the stress area and, wherever possible, to map relationships between them. In the next chapter we shall go on to translate some of these conceptual constructs into more concrete job factors. A narrowing of focus in line with the aims of research will be seen – only the environmental sources of stress and the characteristics of the individual will be treated in depth; the outcomes part of the sequence will be largely ignored.

3 Sources of Managerial Job Stress

Some of the material in this chapter was published in the *Journal of Occupational Psychology*. We would like to thank the BPS for permission to use it.

In this section we will be drawing on literature from three source types:

1. 'Writers', whose works show a largely theoretical basis,
2. 'Company doctors', who from extensive (but usually unquantified) experience of dealing with 'stressed executives' can speak for the particular population they have treated, and
3. Research workers who combine theory with harder 'evidence' in the accepted meaning of the term and therefore will be quoted more extensively.

This material despite its disparate origins is complementary and notably consistent. On examination we find that the factors generated can be grouped neatly under seven main headings – these are shown in Figure 3.1 and will be dealt with in turn.

FACTORS INTRINSIC TO THE JOB

Factors intrinsic to the job were a first and vital focus of study for early researchers in the field and in 'worker' (as opposed to management) studies are still the main preoccupation. Stress can be caused by too much or too little work, time pressures and deadlines, having to make too many decisions (e.g. Sofer, 1970), fatigue from the physical strains of the work environment (e.g. assembly line), excessive travel, long hours, having to cope with changes at work and the expenses (monetary and career) of making mistakes (Kearns, 1973). It can be seen that every job description includes factors which for some individuals at some times will be sources of pressure. Two factors have received the major part of research effort in this area, the others being more speculative rather than proven sources of stress:

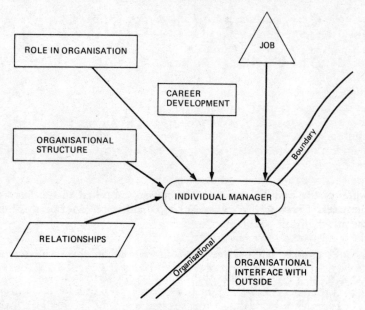

FIGURE 3.1 Sources of managerial job stress

WORKING CONDITIONS

A great deal of work has been done linking the working conditions of a particular job to physical and mental health. Kornhauser (1965) found for example that poor mental health was directly related to unpleasant work conditions, the necessity to work fast and to expend a lot of physical effort, and to excessive and inconvenient hours. There is increasing evidence (Marcson, 1970; Shepard, 1971) that physical health also is adversely affected by repetitive and dehumanising environments (e.g. paced-assembly lines). Kritsikis, Heinemann and Eitner (1968) for example in a study of 150 men with heart disease in a population of over 4000 industrial workers in Berlin reported that a larger number of these workers came from work environments employing conveyor-line systems than any other work technology.

OVERLOAD

Research into work overload has been given substantial empirical attention. French and Caplan (1973) have differentiated overload in terms of *quantitative* and *qualitative* overload. Quantitative refers to having 'too much to do' while qualitative means work that is 'too difficult'. (The complementary phenomena of quantitative and qualitative underload are also hypothesised as potential sources of stress but with little or no supportive research evidence.) Miller (1969) has theorised that 'overload' in most systems leads to breakdown, whether we are dealing with single biological cells or individuals in organisations. In an early study French and Caplan (1970) found that objective quantitative overload was strongly linked to cigarette smoking (a sign of tension and risk factor in CHD). Persons with more phone calls, office visits and meetings per given unit of work time were found to smoke significantly more cigarettes than persons with fewer such engagements. In a study of 100 young coronary patients Russek and Zohman (1958) found that 25% had been working at two jobs and an additional 45% had worked at jobs which required (due to work overload) 60 or more hours per week. They add that although prolonged emotional strain preceded the attack in 91% of the cases similar stress was only observed in 20% of the controls. Breslow and Buell (1960) have also reported findings which support a relationship between hours of work and death from coronary disease. In an investigation of mortality rates of men in California they observed that workers in light industry under the age of 45 who are on the job more than 48 hours a week have twice the risk of death from CHD compared with similar workers working 40 or under hours a week. Another substantial investigation on quantitative workload was carried out by Margolis, Kroes and Quinn (1974) on a representative national sample of 1496 employed persons aged 16 or older. They found that overload was significantly related to a number of symptoms or indicators of stress; escapist drinking, absenteeism from work, low motivation to work, lowered self-esteem and an absence of suggestions to employers. The results from these and other studies (Quinn, Seashore and Mangione, 1971; Porter and Lawler, 1965) are relatively consistent and indicate that this factor is indeed a potential source of occupational stress that affects both health and job satisfaction.

There is also some evidence that (for some occupations) 'qualitative' overload is a source of stress. French, Tupper and Mueller (1965) looked at qualitative and quantitative work overload in a large university. They used questionnaires, interviews and medical examinations to obtain data on risk factors associated with CHD for 122 university administrators and professors. They found that one symptom of stress, low self-esteem, was related to work overload but that this was different for the two occupational groupings. Qualitative overload was not significantly linked to low self-esteem among the administrators but was significantly correlated for the professors. The greater the 'quality' of work expected of the professor the lower the self-esteem. They also found that qualitative and quantitative overload were correlated with achievement orientation. More interestingly it was found in a follow up study that achievement orientation correlated very strongly with serum uric acid (Brooks and Mueller, 1966). Several other studies have reported an association of qualitative work overload with cholesterol level; a tax deadline for accountants (Friedman, Rosenman and Carroll, 1958) and medical students performing a medical examination under observation (Dreyfuss and Czackes, 1959). French and Caplan (1973) summarise this research by suggesting that both qualitative and quantitative overload produce at least nine different symptoms of psychological and physical strain; job dissatisfaction, job tension, lower self-esteem, threat, embarrassment, high cholesterol levels, increased heart rate, skin resistance and more smoking. In analysing this data however one cannot ignore the vital interactive relationship of the job and employee; objective work overload for example should not be viewed in isolation but as relative to the individual's capacities and personality.

Such caution is sanctioned by much of the American and some English literature which shows that overload is not always externally imposed. Many managers (perhaps certain personality types more than others) react to overload by working longer hours. Uris (1972) for example reports on a study in the US in which it was found that 45% of the executives contacted worked all day, in the evenings and at weekends and that a further 37% kept weekends free but worked extra hours in the evenings. In many companies this type of behaviour has become a norm to which everyone feels they must adhere.

ROLE IN THE ORGANISATION

Another major source of occupational stress is associated with a person's role at work. A great deal of research in this area has concentrated on role ambiguity and role conflict since the seminal investigations of the Survey Research Center of the University of Michigan (Kahn *et al.*, 1964).

ROLE AMBIGUITY

Role ambiguity exists when an individual has inadequate information about his work role, that is where there is *lack of clarity* about the work objectives associated with the role, about work colleagues' expectation of the work role and about the scope and responsibilities of the job. Kahn, Wolfe, Quinn, Snoek and Rosenthal (1964) found in their study that men who suffered from role ambiguity experienced lower job satisfaction, high job-related tension, greater futility and lower self-confidence. French and Caplan (1973) found, at one of NASA's bases, in a sample of 205 volunteer engineers, scientists and administrators, that role ambiguity was significantly related to low job satisfaction and to feelings of job-related threat to one's mental and physical well-being. This also related to indicators of physiological strain such as increased blood pressure and pulse rate. Margolis, Kroes and Quinn (1974) also found a number of significant relationships between symptoms or indicators of physical and mental ill-health with role ambiguity in their representative national sample (n = 1496). The stress indicators related to role ambiguity were depressed mood, lowered self-esteem, life dissatisfaction, job dissatisfaction, low motivation to work and intention to leave the job. Whilst these were not very strong statistical relationships they were significant and do indicate that 'lack of role clarity' may be one among many potential stressors at work.

Kahn (1973) feels that it is now time to separate out distinctive elements of role ambiguity for individual treatment (just as he and his research team have done for 'overload' and 'responsibility'). He suggests that two components are involved; those of present- and future-prospects ambiguity (much of the material he assigns to the latter is here classified as career development stress).

ROLE CONFLICT

Role conflict exists when an individual in a particular work role is torn by conflicting job demands or doing things he/she really does not want to do or does not think are part of the job specification. The most frequent manifestation of this is when a person is caught between two groups of people who demand different kinds of behaviour or expect that the job should entail different functions. Kahn *et al.* (1964) found that men who suffered more role conflict had lower job satisfaction and higher job-related tension. It is interesting to note that they also found that the greater the power or authority of the people 'sending' the conflicting role messages the more role conflict produced job dissatisfaction. This was related to physiological strain as well, as the NASA study (French and Caplan, 1970) illustrates. They telemetered and recorded the heart rate of 22 men for a two-hour period while they were at work in their offices. They found that the mean heart rate for an individual was strongly related to his report of role conflict. A larger and medically more sophisticated study by Shirom, Eden, Silberwasser, and Kellerman (1973) found similar results. Their research is of particular interest as it tries to look simultaneously at a wide variety of potential stressors. They collected data on 762 male kibbutz members aged 30 and over drawn from 13 kibbutzim throughout Israel. They examined the relationships between CHD (myocardial infarction, *angina pectoris* and coronary insufficiency), abnormal electrocardiographic readings, CHD risk factors (systolic blood pressure, pulse rate, serum cholesterol levels, etc.) and potential sources of occupational stress (work overload, role ambiguity, role conflict, lack of physical activity). Their data was broken down by occupational groups – agricultural workers, factory groups, craftsmen, and white collar workers. It was found that there was a significant relationship between role conflict and CHD (specifically, abnormal electrocardiographic readings) but for the white collar workers only. In fact as we move down the ladder from occupations requiring greater physical exertion (e.g. agriculture) to less exertion (e.g. white collar) the greater is the relationship between role ambiguity/conflict and abnormal electrocardiographic findings. It was also found that as we go from occupations involving excessive physical activities to those with less such activity, CHD increased significantly. Drawing together this data they concude that clerical, managerial and professional occupations are more likely to suffer occupational stress from identity and other interpersonal problems and less from the physical conditions of work.

A more quantified measure of role conflict itself is found in research reported by Mettlin and Woelfel (1974). They measured three aspects of interpersonal influence-discrepancy between influences, level of influencer and number of influences – in a study of the educational and occupational aspirations of high school students (n = 58). Using the Langner Stress Symptom questionnaire as their index of stress they found that the more extensive and diverse an individual's interpersonal communications network the more stress symptoms he showed.

The organisational role which is at a boundary – i.e. between departments or between the company and the outside world – is by definition one of high role conflict. Kahn *et al.* (1964) cite such a position as being potentially very stressful. They quote no research evidence however to show whether an individual in it copes more or less well with conflict than other managers as a result of its being a basic component of his job-description. Other researchers have also cited the boundary position as one of high stress potential: Margolis and Kroes (1974) for example report that foremen are seven times as likely to develop ulcers as shop-floor workers.

RESPONSIBILITY

Another important potential stressor associated with one's organisational role is 'responsibility'. One can differentiate here between 'responsibility for people' and 'responsibility for things' (equipment, budgets, etc.). Wardwell, Hyman and Bahnson (1964) found that responsibility for people was significantly more likely to lead to CHD than responsibility for things. Increased responsibility for people frequently means that one has to spend more time interacting with others, attending meetings, working alone and in consequence, as in the Goddard study (French and Caplan, 1970), more time in trying to meet deadline pressure and schedules. Pincherle (1972) also found this in a UK study of 2000 executives attending a medical centre for a medical check-up. Of the 1200 managers sent by their companies for their annual examination there was evidence of physical stress being linked to age and level of responsibility; the older and more responsible the executive, the greater the probability of the presence of CHD risk factors or symptoms. The relationship between age and stress-related illness could be explained however by the fact that as the executive gets older he may be troubled by stressors other than increased responsibility. These, as Eaton (1969) suggests, might be (1) a recognition that further advancement is unlikely (2) increasing isolation and narrowing of interests and (3) an awareness of approaching retirement. Nevertheless the finding by French and Caplan in the NASA study does indicate that responsibility for people must play some part in the process of stress particularly for clerical, managerial and professional workers. They found that responsibility for people was significantly related to heavy smoking, diastolic blood pressure and serum cholesterol levels. The more the individual had responsibility for things as opposed to people the lower were each of these CHD risk factors.

OTHERS

Having too little responsibility (Brook, 1973), lack of participation in decision-making, lack of managerial support, having to keep up with increasing standards of performance and coping with rapid technological change are other potential role stresses mentioned repeatedly in the literature but with little supportive research evidence. Variations between organisational structures will determine the differential distribution of these across differing occupational groups. Kay (1974) does suggest however that independent of the particular characteristics of the employing organisation some pressures are to be found more at middle than at other management levels. He depicts today's middle manager as being particularly hard pressed:

1. by pay compression, as the salaries of new recruits increase.
2. by job insecurity – they are particularly vulnerable to redundancy or forced, premature retirement.
3. by having little *real* authority at their high levels of responsibility.
4. by feeling 'boxed-in'.

When interviewed it is those pressures intrinsic to the job and due to role in organisation which managers consider to be the most legitimate sources of stress vis-à-vis their jobs. Typically they are referred to as 'what I'm paid for', 'why I'm here', and even when they cause severe disruption, the implication is that they cannot be legitimately avoided. In many companies in fact there are institutional ways in which these problems can be handled; for example deadlines are set unrealistically

early to allow a margin of error, decisions are made by groups so that
no one individual has to take full responsibility, the employee is allowed
to neglect certain tasks (e.g. filing) if he is busy and work can be
reallocated within a department if one member is seen to be doing more
than his fair share. The manager however may not always perceive
himself as free to use these fail-safe mechanisms.

RELATIONSHIPS AT WORK

'Pas besoin de gril: l'enfer, c'est les Autres'
Jean-Paul Sartre, 1947

A third major source of stress at work has to do with the nature of
relationships with one's boss, subordinates and colleagues. A number of
behavioural scientists (Argyris, 1964; Cooper, 1973) have suggested that
good relationships between members of a work group are a central factor in individual and organisational health. Nevertheless very little
research work has been done in this area either to support or disprove
this hypothesis. French and Caplan (1973) define poor relations as
'those which include low trust, low supportiveness and low interest in
listening to and trying to deal with problems that confront the
organisational member.' The most notable studies in this area are by
Kahn *et al.* (1964), French and Caplan (1970) and Buck (1972). Both the
Kahn *et al.* and French and Caplan studies came to roughly the same
conclusion that mistrust of persons one worked with was positively
related to high role ambiguity which led to inadequate communications
between people and to 'psychological strain in the form of low job
satisfaction and to feelings of job-related threat to one's well being.' It
was interesting to note however in the Kahn *et al.* study that poor
relations with one's subordinates was significantly related to feelings of
threat with colleagues and superiors but not in relationship to threat
with subordinates.

RELATIONSHIP WITH SUPERIOR

Buck (1972) focused on the attitude and relationship of workers and
managers to their immediate boss using Fleishman's leadership
questionnaire on consideration and initiating structure. The consideration factor was associated with behaviour indicative of friendship,
mutual trust, respect and a certain warmth between boss and subordinate. He found that those workers who felt that their boss was low on
'consideration' reported feeling more job pressure. Workers who were
under pressure reported that their boss did not give them criticism in a
helpful way, played favourites with subordinates and ' "pulled rank"
and took advantage of them whenever they got a chance'. Buck con-

cludes that the 'lack of considerate behaviour of supervisors appears to have contributed significantly to feelings of job pressure.'

RELATIONSHIPS WITH SUBORDINATES

Officially one of the most critical functions of a manager is his supervision of other people's work. It has long been accepted that an 'inability to delegate' might be a problem but now a new strain is being put on the manager's interpersonal skills – he must learn to govern by participation. Donaldson and Gowler (1975) point to the factors which may make today's zealous emphasis on participation a cause of resentment, anxiety and stress for the manager concerned:

1. mismatch of formal and actual powers
2. the manager may well resent the erosion of his formal role and powers (and the loss of status and rewards)
3. he may be subject to irreconcilable pressures – e.g. to be both participative and to achieve high production
4. his subordinates may refuse to participate.

Particularly for those with technical and scientific backgrounds (a 'things-orientation') relationships can be a low priority (seen as 'trivial', 'petty', time-consuming and an impediment to doing the job well) and one would expect their interactions to be more a source of stress than those of people-oriented managers.

RELATIONSHIPS WITH COLLEAGUES

Besides the obvious factors of office politics and colleague rivalry, we find another element here: stress can be caused not only by the press of relationships but also by the opposite – a lack of adequate social support in difficult situations (Lazarus, 1966). At highly competitive managerial levels it is likely that problem-sharing will be inhibited for fear of appearing weak and much of the literature (American in particular) mentions the isolated life of the top executive as an added source of strain.

Morris (1975) encompasses this whole area of relationships in one model which he calls the 'cross of relationships'.

Whilst he acknowledges the differences between relationships on the various arms he feels that the focal manager must bring all four into 'dynamic balance' in order to be able to deal with the stress of his position. Morris's suggestion seems 'only sensible' when we see how much of his work time the manager does spend with other people. In a research programme designed to find out exactly what managers do Minzberg (1973) showed just how much of their time is spent in interaction. In an intensive study of a small sample of chief executives he found

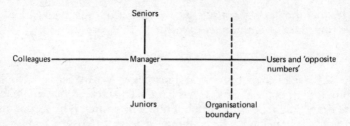

FIGURE 3.2 The cross of relationships

that in a large organisation a mere 22% of time was spent in desk work sessions, the rest being taken up by telephone calls (6%), scheduled meetings (59%), unscheduled meetings (10%) and other activities (3%). In small organisations basic desk work played a larger part (52%) but nearly 40% was still devoted to face-to-face contacts of one kind or another.

Despite its obvious importance and the inclusion of 'relationship measures' in many multivariate studies there is little depth material available in this area.

CAREER DEVELOPMENT

Two major clusters of potential stressors can be identified in this area: (1) lack of job security – fear of redundancy, obsolescence or early retirement, and (2) status incongruity, e.g. under- or over-promotion, frustration at having reached one's career ceiling. (Much of the material relating to the latter has already been dealt with in Chapter 2 in the section on Mobility and Status Incongruence.)

For many managers their career progression is of overriding importance – by promotion they earn not only money but enhanced status and the new job challenges for which they strive. Typically in the early years at work this striving and the aptitude to come to terms quickly with a rapidly changing environment is fostered and suitably rewarded by the company. Career progression is perhaps a problem by its nature (Sofer (1970) found that many of his sample believed that 'luck' and 'being in the right place at the right time' play a major role) but it does nonetheless occur. At middle age, and usually middle-management levels, career becomes more problematic and most executives find their progress slowed, if not actually stopped. Job opportunities become fewer, those jobs that are available take longer to master, past (mistaken?) decisions cannot be revoked, old knowledge and methods become obsolete, energies may be flagging or demanded for family activities and there is the 'press' of fresh young recruits to face in competition. Both Levinson (1973) and Constandse (1972) – the latter refers to this phase as 'the male menopause' – depict the manager as suffering these fears and disappointments in silent isolation from his family and work colleagues.

The fear of demotion or obsolescence can be strong for those who know they have reached their career ceiling – and most will inevitably suffer some erosion of status before they finally retire. Goffman (1952), extrapolating from a technique employed in the con-game ('cooling the mark out'), suggests that the company should bear some of the responsibility for taking the sting out of this (felt) failure experience.

From the company perspective on the other hand McMurray (1973a) puts the case for not promoting to a higher position if there is doubt that the employee can fill it. In a syndrome he labels 'the executive neurosis', he describes the over-promoted manager as grossly overworking to keep down a top job, and at the same time hide his insecurity, and points to the consequences of this for his work performance and the company. Age is no longer revered as it was – it is becoming a 'young man's world'. The rapidity with which society is developing (technologically, economically and socially) is likely to mean that individuals will now need to change career during their working life (as companies and products are having to do). Such trends breed uncertainty and research suggests that older workers look for stability (Sleeper, 1975). Unless managers adapt their expectations to suit new circumstances career development stress, especially in later life, is likely to become an increasingly common experience.

ORGANISATIONAL STRUCTURE AND CLIMATE

A fifth potential source of organisational stress is simply 'being in the organisation' and the threat to an individual's freedom, autonomy and identity this poses. Criticisms such as little or no participation in the decison-making process, no sense of belonging, lack of effective consultation and communication, restrictions on behaviour (e.g. budgets), office politics will be appropriate here. An increasing number of research investigations are being conducted in this area, particularly into the effect of employee participation in the workplace. This research development is contemporaneous to a growing movement in North America and in the EEC countries of worker participation programmes, involving autonomous work groups, worker-directors, and a greater sharing of the decision-making process throughout the organisation. The early work on participation was in terms of its effect on production and attitudes of workers. For example Coch and French (1948) examined the degrees of participation in a sewing factory. They found the greater the participation the higher was the productivity, the greater the job satisfaction the lower the turnover and the better were the relationships between boss and subordinate. These findings were later supported by a field experiment in a footwear factory in Southern Norway where greater participation led to significantly more favourable attitudes by workers toward management and more involvement in their jobs (French, Israel and As, 1960).

The research more relevant to our interests here however is the recent work on lack of participation and stress-related disease. In the NASA study (French and Caplan, 1970) for example it was found that people who reported greater opportunities for participation in decision-making reported significantly greater job satisfaction, low job-related feelings of threat and higher feelings of self-esteem. Buck (1972) found that both managers and workers who felt 'under pressure' most reported that their supervisors 'always ruled with an iron hand and rarely tried out new ideas or allowed participation in decision-making.' Managers who were under stress also reported that their supervisors never let the persons under them do their work in the way they thought best. Margolis, Kroes, & Quinn (1974) found that 'non-participation at work' was the most consistent and significant predictor or indicator of strain and job-related stress. They found that non-participation was significantly related to the following health risk factors: overall poor physical health, escapist drinking, depressed mood, low self-esteem, low life satisfaction, low job satisfaction, low motivation to work, intention to leave job and absenteeism from work. Kasl (1973) also found that low job satisfaction was related to non-participation in decision-making, inability to provide feedback to supervisors and lack of recognition for good performance; and that poor mental health was linked to close supervision and no autonomy at work (Quinn, Seashore and Mangione, 1971). Neff (1968) has highlighted the importance of lack of participation and involvement by suggesting the 'mental health at work is to a large extent a function of the degree to which output is under the control of the individual worker.' To summarise, the research above seems to indicate that greater participation leads to lower staff turnover and higher productivity and that when participation is absent lower job satisfaction and higher levels of physical and mental health risks result.

We have seen (Donaldson and Gowler, 1975) however that it may be difficult to satisfy the needs of all levels of the workforce with the same change programme. There is therefore reason to approach this topic with caution particularly as the studies quoted relied on correlational analysis for their conclusions and the inferences as to causality that can be drawn are limited.

EXTRA-ORGANISATIONAL SOURCES OF STRESS

The sixth and final 'source' of external job stress is more a 'catch-all' for all those exchanges between his life outside and his life inside the organisation that might put pressure on the manager – family problems (Pahl and Pahl. 1971), life crises (Dohrenwend and Dohrenwend, 1974), financial difficulties, conflict of personal beliefs with those of the company and the conflict of company with family demands. Despite repeated calls for researchers to acknowledge that the individual 'functions as a totality' (Wright, 1975b), the practical problems of encompassing the whole person in one research plan usually leave those who try with either incomprehensibly complex results or platitudinous generalisations. Most studies then have only one life area as the focus of study.

The area which has received most research interest is that of the manager's relationship with his wife and family. (It is widely agreed that managers have little time for 'outside activities' apart from their families. Writers who have examined their effects on the local community (e.g. Packard, 1975) have pointed to the disruptive effects of the executive's *lack* of participation.)

The manager has two main problems vis-à-vis his family:

1. The first is that of time – and commitment – management. Not only does his busy life leave him few resources to cope with other people's needs but in order to do his job well the manager usually also needs support from others to cope with the 'background' details of house management, etc, to relieve stress when possible and to maintain contact with the outside world, and

2. The second, often a result of the first, is the spill-over of crises or stresses in one system to affect the other.

As these two are inseparable we shall go on to discuss them together.

MARRIAGE PATTERNS

The 'arrangement' the manager comes to with his wife will be of vital importance to both problem areas. Pahl and Pahl (1971) found that the majority of wives in their middle-class sample saw their role in relation to their husband's job as a supportive, domestic one; all said that they derived their sense of security from their husbands (only two men said the same of their wives). Barber (1976) interviewing five directors' wives finds similar attitudes. Gowler and Legge (1975) have dubbed this bond 'the hidden contract' in which the wife agrees to act as a 'supportive team' so that her husband can fill the demanding job to which he aspires. Handy (1975) supports the idea that this is 'typical' and that it is the path to career success for the manager concerned. Based on individual psychometric data he describes four possible marriage-role combinations. In his sample of top British executives in mid-career and their wives he found that the most frequent pattern (about half the twenty-two couples interviewed) was the thrusting male-caring female.

This he depicts as highly role segregated with the emphasis on 'separation', 'silence' and complementary activities. Historically both the company and the manager have reaped benefits from maintaining the segregation of work and home implicit in this pattern. The company thus legitimates its demands for a constant work performance from its employee, no matter what his home situation, and the manager is free to pursue his career but keeps a safe haven to which he can return to relax and recuperate. The second most frequent combination involved a dual-career pattern with the emphasis on complete sharing. This, whilst potentially fulfilling for both parties, requires energy inputs which might well prove so excessive that none of the roles involved are filled successfully.

It is unlikely that the patterns described above will usually be negotiated explicitly or that they will be in a long-term balance. Major factors in their continuing evolution will be the work and family demands of particular life stages. A recent report by the BIM, The Management Threshold (Beattie, Darlington and Cripps, 1974), for example highlights the difficult situation of the young executive who in order to build up his career must devote a great deal of time and energy to his job just when his young housebound wife with small children is also making pressing demands. The report suggests that the executive fights to maintain the distance between his wife and the organisation so that she will not be in a position to evaluate the choices he has to make; paradoxically he does so at a time when he is most in need of sympathy and understanding. Guest and Williams (1973) look at the complete career-cycle in similar terms pointing out how the demands of the different systems change over time. The addition of role- and personality-disposition variations to their 'equations' would however make them even more valuable.

MOBILITY

The manager's work:home conflicts become particularly critical in relation to moving. Much of the literature on this topic comes from the United States where mobility is much more a part of the national character than in the UK (Pierson, 1972) but there is reason to believe that here too it is an increasingly common phenomena.

At an individual level the effects of mobility on the manager's wife and family have been studied. Researchers agree that whether she is willing to go or not the wife bears the brunt of moving. They conclude that most husbands do not appreciate what this involves. American writers point to signs that wives are suffering and becoming less cooperative. Immundo (1974) hypothesises that increasing divorce rates are seen as the upwardly aspiring manager races ahead of his socially unskilled, 'stay-at-home' wife. Seidenberg (1973) comments on the rise in the ratio of female to male alcoholics in the United States from 1:5 in 1972 to 1:3 in 1973 and asks the question 'Do corporate wives have souls?' Descriptive accounts of the frustrations and loneliness of being a 'corporate wife' in the US and UK proliferate. Increasing teenage delinquency and violence is also laid at the door of the mobile manager and the society which he has created.

Constant moving can have profound effects on the life style of the people concerned – particularly on their relationships with others. Staying only two years or so in one place mobile families do not have time to develop close ties with the local community. Immundo (1974) talks of the 'mobility syndrome', a way of behaving geared to developing only temporary relationships. Packard (1975) describes ways in which individuals react to the type of fragmenting society this creates: e.g. treating everything as if it is temporary, being indifferent to local community amenities and organisations, living for the present and becoming adept at 'instant gregariousness'. He goes on to point out the likely consequences for local communities, the nation and the rootless people involved.

Pahl and Pahl (1971) suggest that the British reaction is characteristically more reserved and that many mobiles retreat into their nuclear family. This conclusion is supported, at a theoretical level, by Parsons (1943) who is concerned that even greater demands for stability, identity and emotional support are placed on this, already often precarious, institution. Managers particularly do not become involved in local affairs due both to lack of time and to an appreciation that they are only 'short-stay' inhabitants. Their wives find participation easier (especially in a mobile rather than static area) and a recent survey on Middle Class Housing Estates (*The Times*, 1975) suggested that for some involvement is a necessity to compensate for their husband's ambitions and career involvement which keep him away from home.

From the company's point of view the way in which a wife does adjust to her new environment can feedback to her husband's work performance. Guest and Williams (1973) illustrate this by an example of a major international company who on surveying 1800 of their executives in 70 countries concluded that the two most important influences on overall satisfaction with the overseas assignment were the job itself and the wives' adjustment to the foreign environment. Clinical evidence suggesting that one partner's problems may even contribute to the mental ill-health of the other comes from work at Edinburgh University (e.g. Kreitman, 1968).

Despite the importance of the work:home interface and the real problem that it poses to almost all managers and their wives at some time or another there is a distinct lack of work to suggest how conflict effects both work performance and marriage or how crises or triumphs in one system feed back to influence the other.

CHARACTERISTICS OF THE INDIVIDUAL

Sources of pressure at work evoke different reactions from different people. Some people are better able to cope with these stressors than others; they adapt their behaviour in a way that meets the environmental challenge. On the other hand some personality types seem more predisposed to stress; that is they are unable to cope or adapt to the stress-provoking situation. Many factors may contribute to these differences – personality, motivation, being well- or ill-equipped to deal with problems in a particular area of expertise, fluctuations in abilities (particularly with age), insight into ones own motivations and weaknesses, etc. It is necessary to look therefore at those characteristics of the individual that are predisposers to stress in order to round off this discussion. Most of the research in this area has been directed at personality; having discussed this we shall look briefly at some 'self-help' literature that is also appropriate here.

There have been two principal directions of research into personality: one has concentrated on examining the relationship between various psychometric measures (primarily using the MMPI and 16PF) and stress-related disease (primarily CHD); the other has considered stress- or coronary-prone behaviour patterns and the incidence of disease. Jenkins (1971a, 1971b) provides an extensive review of these studies.

PSYCHOMETRIC MEASURES

In the first category there were six studies which utilised the MMPI. The result of these six studies (Bakker and Levenson, 1967; Ostfeld, Lebovits and Shekelle, 1964; Lebovits, Shekelle and Ostfeld, 1967; Brozek, Keys and Blackburn, 1966; Bruhn, Chandler and Wolf, 1969; Mordkoff and Rand, 1968) seems to be that before their illness patients with coronary disease differ from persons who remain healthy on several MMPI scales, particularly those in the 'neurotic' triad of hypochondriasis (Hs), depression (D) and hysteria (Hy). The occurrence of manifest CHD increases the deviation of patients' MMPI scores further and in addition there is ego defence breakdown. As Jenkins (1971a) summarises: 'Patients with fatal disease tend to show greater neuroticism (particularly depression) in prospective MMPI's than those who incur and survive coronary disease.' There are three major studies utilising the 16PF (Bakker, 1967; Finn, Hickey and O'Doherty, 1969; Lebovits, Shekelle and Ostfeld, 1967). All three of these report emotional instability (low Scale C) particularly for patients with *angina pectoris*. Two studies report high conformity and submissiveness (Factor E) and desurgency/seriousness (Factor F); two report high self-sufficiency (Factor Q2). Bakker's *angina* patients are similar to Finn's sample with CHD in manifesting shyness (Factor H) and apprehensiveness (Factor D). The results from all three studies portray the patients with CHD or related illness as emotionally unstable and introverted which is consistent with the six MMPI studies. The limitation of these studies is that they are on balance retrospective; anxiety and neuroticism may well be reactions to CHD and other stress-related illnesses rather than precursors of it. Paffenbarger, Wolf and Notkin (1966) did an interesting prospective study in which they linked university psychometric data on students with death certificates filed years later. They found a number of significant precursors to fatal CHD, one of which was a high anxiety/neuroticism score for the fatal cases.

Kahn *et al.* (1964) adopting a more selective approach to personality measurement came up with some more practically oriented results than those of the above general explorations. They examined a sample of managers on a series of personality variables; extroversion versus introversion, flexibility versus rigidity, inner- versus out-directedness, open- versus closed-mindedness, achievement/status versus security oriented. They then related these to job stress. The following gives an indication of some of their results: (1) outer-directed people were more adaptable and more highly reality-oriented than inner-directed; (2) 'rigids' and 'flexibles' perceived different types of situations as stressful, the former being more susceptible to rush jobs from above and dependence on other people whilst the latter were more open to influence from other people and thus easily became overloaded; (3) achievement-seekers showed significantly more independence and job involvement than did security-seekers.

BEHAVIOUR PATTERNS

The other research approach to individual stress differences began with the work of Friedman and Rosenman (Friedman, 1969; Rosenman, Friedman and Strauss, 1964, 1966) in the early sixties and developed later showing a relationship between behavioural patterns and the prevalence of CHD. They found that individuals manifesting certain behavioural traits were significantly more at risk to CHD. These individuals were later referred to as the 'coronary-prone behaviour pattern Type A' as distinct from Type B (low risk of CHD). Type A was found to be the overt behavioural syndrome or style of living characterised by 'extremes of competitiveness, striving for achievement, oppressiveness, haste, impatience, restlessness, hyper- alertness, explosiveness of speech, tenseness of facial musculature and feelings of being under pressure of time and under the challenge of responsibility'. It was suggested that 'people having this particular behavioural pattern were often so deeply involved and committed to their work that other aspects of their lives were relatively neglected' (Jenkins, 1971b). In the early studies persons were designated as Type A or Type B on the basis of clinical judgements by doctors and psychologists or peer ratings. These studies found higher incidence of CHD among Type A than Type B. Many of the inherent methodological weaknesses of this approach were overcome by the classic Western Collaborative Group Study (Rosenman, Friedman and Strauss, 1964, 1966). It was a prospective (as opposed to the earlier retrospective studies) national study of over 3400 men free of CHD. All these men were rated Type A or B by psychiatrists after intensive interviews without having knowledge of any biological data about them and without the individuals being seen by a cardiologist. Diagnosis was made by an electrocardiographer and in-dependent medical internist who were not informed about the subjects' behavioural patterns. They found the following results after $2\frac{1}{2}$ years from the start of the study, Type A men between the ages of 39 and 49 and 50 and 59, had 6.5 and 1.9 times respectively the incidence of CHD as compared with Type B men. They also had the following risk factors of elevated serum cholesterol levels, elevated beta-lipoproteins, decreased blood clotting time and elevated daytime excretion of norepinephrine. After $4\frac{1}{2}$ years of the follow-up observation in the study the *same* relationship of behavioural pattern and incidence of CHD was found. In terms of the clinical manifestations of CHD individuals exhibiting Type A behavioural patterns had significantly more incidence of acute myocardial infarction (and of clinically unrecognised myocar-dial infarction) and *angina pectoris*. Rosenman, Friedman and Jenkins (1967) also found that the risk of recurrent and fatal myocardial infarc-tion was significantly related to Type A characteristics. Quinlan and his colleagues (Quinlan, Burrow and Hayes, 1969) found the same results among Trappist and Benedictine monks. Monks judged to be Type A coronary-prone cases (by a double-blind procedure) had 2.3 times the prevalence of *angina* and 4.3 times the prevalence of infarction as com-pared to monks judged to be Type B. Many other studies (Bortner and Rosenman, 1967; Zyzanski and Jenkins, 1970) have been conducted with roughly the same findings.

Researchers at the Institute of Social Research, University of Michigan have focused on A-type characteristics as the sole personality measure in many of their studies. Sales (1969) developed a 49-item questionnaire test of Type A; a nine-item rationalisation is now also available (Vickers, 1973). Using the Sales version Caplan *et al.*, (1975) found no significant correlations between personality 'pure' and the 'strains' measured (job dissatisfaction, somatic complaints, anxiety, depression, irritation, physical and behavioural 'stress' correlates). Their expectation to find relationships at interactive levels instead is borne out by previous research experience. Caplan and Jones (1975) for example report on the mediating role of personality. In their study of 73 male users of a university computer system in the 'stressful' time before a 23-day shutdown they found confirmation of previous findings that role ambiguity was positively associated with anxiety, depression and resentment and workload with anxiety, but report that these relationships were greatest for Type A personalities.

In a further study by Caplan, Cobb and French (1975), the team investigated the relationship between smoking and A-type personality and shed light on 'A's' ability to modify his coronary-prone behaviour. Caplan *et al.* report that only a fifth of those who try to give up smoking are successful. Following a questionnaire survey of 2000 administrators, engineers and scientists at NASA they tried to relate 'quitting' to job stress, personality and social support. They found that 'quitters' had the lowest levels on quantitative workload, responsibility and social support and that they scored low on Type A characteristics. Care must be taken in interpreting these correlational results (it may well be that Type As seek out high workloads, etc.). One conclusion can however be drawn unequivocally: A-type personalities are less likely to give up smoking than are B-types (as the authors point out over time this will lead to an increase in the association between smoking and risk of CHD); thus it would appear that the former's characteristics are so fundamental that they are unable to help themselves (if helped they must be!). Payne (1975) has this in mind when he expresses the need (in somewhat rarefied tones) for social systems of trust and support which would 'manipulate the degree of environmental pressures so as to give a pinprick to the comfortable B-types and respite to the harassed As'.

Further confirmation of the legitimacy of the behaviour-pattern approach comes from the two final studies to be mentioned here. The first started from a more basic level than that outlined above by taking a check-list of 25 'habits of nervous tension' (Thomas and Ross, 1967). The 1085 medical student subjects were asked to tick those which corresponded to their reactions when 'in situations of undue pressure or stress'. Whilst highly individual patterns of response were found it was possible:

(1) to derive eight factors (by factor analysis) from the total twenty-five items – these were 'activity', 'appetite', 'irritation', 'visceral reaction', 'general stress', 'dependency', 'compulsivity' and 'stimulation' and suggest dimensions on which to base further research, and

(2) to relate individual items to serum cholesterol levels – five items were significantly different for high and low cholesterol groups. Low cholesterol subjects more often reported loss of appetite, exhaustion, nausea and anxiety and high cholesterol subjects an urge to eat.

The second study is much more assumptive in approach. Gemill and Heisler (1972) set out to investigate the relationship between

'Machiavellianism' (a tendency to manipulate and persuade others, to
initiate and control in group situations and generally 'be a winner'), job
strain, job satisfaction, positional mobility and perceived opportunities
for formal control. High Machiavellian scorers were overall much less
happy in their jobs – showing more job strain, less satisfaction and
lower perceived opportunities for formal control – than low scorers.
Explanation of these results is not easy (largely because the researchers
failed to reach the underlying elements in a complex situation). These
differences could be (1) perceptual, due to a basic Machiavellian
cynacism; (2) because of the subjects' ways of operating which are likely
to cause them frustration or (3) because they worked for formalised
organisations and not in the ambiguous environments in which they
flourish.

To summarise whilst psychometric measures do show relationships
with stress measures the macro-approach of behaviour patterns offers
more practically applicable data. One is able, happily, to retain the advantages of both approaches by using the former for their sensitivity but
looking for the emergence of the latter in the patterning of results.

A research technique which stands somewhat alone by explicitly incorporating personal characteristics into job stress measures (and at the
same time reduces the number of variables in, and therefore the complexity of, multivariate analysis) is discussed by Van Harrison (1975) and
French (1973). They assess 'person–environment fit' by asking subjects
to indicate desired and 'actual' levels of workload, work complexity,
responsibility, ambiguity, etc. in their jobs and then taking the
difference between scores on the various dimensions as their measures.
(Some other questionnaires do contain this evaluative element im-
plicitly.) This approach has been relatively successful and P-E fit has
proved to be an equally good or more powerful predictor of strain (job
dissatisfaction, anxiety, depression etc.) than either elements separately
(although there are still some 'unsolved problems of analysis').

'SELF-HELP' LITERATURE

Given that work is stressful and that some people are more susceptible
to stress diseases than are others a considerable body of literature is
aimed at helping the individual manager minimise his risks and still do
the job.

Wright (1975b) deals comprehensively with this topic pointing out the
role that the wife and family can play. Others have focused on specific
aspects such as early diagnosis (Wright, 1967), exercise (Perham, 1972;
Bellotto, 1971), biofeedback (Levy, 1973) and relaxation by
transcendental meditation (Clutterbuck, 1973). That such measures can
be effective is shown by the report (Doyle, 1975) that risk of heart disease
is being successfully reduced for the 10,000 experimental subjects (ver-

sus 10,000 controls) in a prospective Swedish community study. The subjects were given treatment or advice about 'healthier living' with the emphasis on diet and smoking.

SUMMARY AND CONCLUSIONS

Drawing together Chapters 2 and 3, the literature reviews of the stress field in general and managerial stress in particular, we find that the area of managerial job pressure is in fact very poorly researched and that the body of work which has been done is deficient in certain important ways:

1. Few studies treat job stress comprehensively. Typically the focus is on a small range of potential stressors – e.g. role conflict and role ambiguity or job content. Whilst this approach has many benefits, especially in the early 'definition-of-concepts' stages, it is not an adequate base for a full understanding of an individual's work experience.

2. A second sign of the failure to treat man as a totality is the attempt to study 'stress' in isolation from the rest of working life, particularly from those elements which contribute to job satisfaction. We see how unrealistic such an approach is from the above section on job stress. Almost everything in the work situation has been identified as a pressure by someone, at sometime; frequently both a situation and its direct opposite can cause stress – e.g. overwork and underwork – and many of the potential stresses quoted have elsewhere been cited as direct or indirect sources of job satisfaction – a 'poorly defined task' for example whilst causing anxiety can also provide scope for the worker to use his initiative and gain greater satisfaction from performing well. To look only for the negative effects of a particular stimulus is to deny (and usually to confirm) that any other outcomes are possible.

3. Even if 'working-man' is to be separated out from 'home-man' as an accessible, researchable entity there are several intuitively important 'interface' variables which researchers usually fail to take into account – e.g. How important is the job relative to the employee's other life areas? Is the work:home balance different at different stages of the life cycle? Do the manager's wife and family make demands on him that conflict with those made by the company?

4. Much of the research on job stress has been internally self-validating – potential stressors are decided on by investigators and included in questionnaires which are then used as measures of stress. Little attention has been paid to finding out if the con-

stituent items really are sources of stress or if pressures of different strengths and types can be identified.

5. We have seen that there is theoretical agreement that stress is perceptually defined; often however researchers try to assess stress objectively (e.g. a particular situation or number of hours worked) and without recourse to the interpretation made by the individual concerned.

6. The failure of many to base their research on adequate interactive conceptual models has played a major part in the confusing of dependent and independent variables and the complete failure to include other dimensions noted in 1 to 5 above.

7. Whilst they will admit in discussion that stress is part of a dynamic long-term interaction between organism and environment most researchers use correlational analysis rather than longitudinal study as a basis for causal inference. The former has several serious drawbacks in such a context. The significant correlation of two variables – low job level and lack of job satisfaction to give a typical example – is just as likely to mean that:

   a. low job level leads to low job satisfaction as that
   b. low job satisfaction results in behaviour which keeps the employee at a low job level as that
   c. the two variables are related but due to a third factor –e.g. lack of education – as that
   d. the two variables are only loosely related and part of a much wider syndrome – e.g. 'the drop-out mentality' as that
   e. it is just a 'coincidence' in the popular sense of the term.

The decision to choose interpretation (a) should be, but is not always, justified by substantiating evidence from other sources.

8. Studies have been either small-scale or large-scale but on mixed populations. In an area in which individual differences play such a vital part both small and heterogeneous samples must be treated with caution.

9. Managers have been largely neglected as a target for quantified study (a high percentage of the managerial literature that does exist is either conceptual or anecdotal). The results of the one major study in which managers were questioned extensively (Buck, 1972) were used to compare this group to shop-floor workers rather than to look at their pressure *per se*.

In terms of both content and concept therefore past studies are open to improvement. In the chapter that follows we will describe a large scale study carried out by the authors to assess the sources of managerial stress which we hope has minimised some of these methodological problems.

4   A Systematic Investigation of Managerial Stress

Figure 4.1 shows the conceptual model of job stress on which this research was based. A review of the literature (Chapter 3) revealed a formidable list of factors identified by one or another researcher or writer as causes of stress (Cooper and Marshall, 1975a). Almost every dimension of working life is a source of stress to someone at sometime. Often a situation and its direct opposite are both potential causes of stress – e.g. overload (Quinn, Seashore and Mangione, 1971; French and Caplan, 1973) *and* underload (Zuckerman, Levine and Biase, 1964), underpromotion (Morris, 1956) *and* overpromotion (Brook, 1973; Arthur and Gunderson, 1965). In Figure 4.1 all the various factors are categorised under seven general headings, six 'external' and one 'internal' to the individual concerned. Whilst the content speaks for itself two structural factors deserve mention as they made key contributions to the conceptualisation and methodology eventually adopted:

1. It appears that stress is not a characteristic of either environment or individual but is the outcome of the interaction of the two. Lazarus (1971) has emphasised that it is a person's perception of a situation, his 'cognitive appraisal', which defines it as stressful: 'the (stress) reaction depends on how the person interprets or appraises (consciously or unconsciously) the significance of a harmful, threatening or challenging event.' Appley (1962) uses the term 'threat perception' to designate this, the most important, link between objective circumstance and the human experience of stress. Stress appears then to be a matter of Person:Environment fit (P:E fit for short); the research design model takes this as a basic assumption with a view to substantiating it by research. In line with this conceptualisation stress is regarded as *a state of the organism* which is the outcome of a particular combination of P with E; it can be recognised by its symptoms (anxiety, feeling that one is unable to cope, physical manifestations, etc.). To make the distinction clear the terms 'pressure' and 'stressor' are used to refer to the elements which contribute causatively (and interactively) to this

Elements found to be associated with stress:

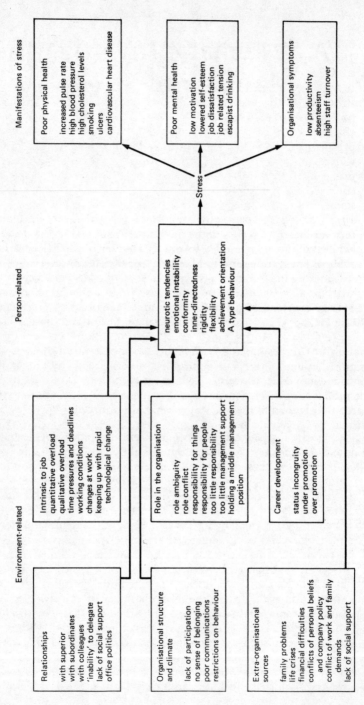

FIGURE 4.1 The P:E fit model applied to managerial job stress

outcome (these are shown on the left-hand side of Diagram 1). These can be stimuli to growth and achievement or a source of stress depending on how they are perceived and dealt with.

2. It also became evident that there is a close association between stress and satisfaction: almost all the potential stressors are also potential sources of satisfaction either in the long-term (facing a challenge may be uncomfortable at the time but is a necessary precursor to the feelings of growth and achievement which come with success) or the short-term (ambiguous organisational roles may cause their holders many problems but usually they also offer considerable opportunities for autonomy). Physiologically too the states are closely similar (Froberg, Karlsson, Levi and Lidberg, 1971; Mills, 1976). It was therefore decided to ask managers about the satisfactions (as well as the pressures) involved in their jobs (whilst still focusing more on stress as the outcome) in order to achieve a comprehensive view of their experiences of working life.

METHODS: QUALITATIVE AND QUANTITATIVE DATA COLLECTION

We should like now to describe how the research model was operationalised and how these conceptual considerations were catered for in the study. Data was collected between December 1974 and October 1975 from the senior managers of a multinational company and some of their wives. Fieldwork was conducted in two phases: the first consisted of individual, in depth interviews with 55 managers and 40 managers' wives spread over four of the company's sites (Head Office and three others). Each interview lasted over an hour and covered chiefly:

the manager's work history
the effects of any moves he had made on himself and his family
the pressures and satisfactions in his current job
the most stressful and satisfying times in his past career
his attitudes to his career development so far and his future prospects
the role his wife adopts in relation to his work including her own career, if any.

This material was used both as data in its own right and as a basis for the development of a second, quantitative phase of study. In order to acquire supplementary, statistically-analysable data from which more confident generalisations could be made a questionnaire package was then put together and circulated to 208 senior managers (wives were not included in this phase of study). The overwhelming majority of these were contacted personally or by telephone with a view to ensuring that all understood the aims of the study and to give them an opportunity to ask any questions about it. The final response rate of 89% shows the value of adopting such an approach.

The questionnaire package was designed specifically to operationalise the elements of the underlying research model introduced above. Figure 4.2 fills the model out in these 'concrete' terms. On the left-hand side are the hypothesised causes of stress, the independent variables in the analysis which follow and on the right-hand side, the criteria measures of stress, the dependent variables selected for this study. Questions were asked about the two main categories of person-related variables which might contribute to causing stress:

i. the individual's personal demographics – age, lifestage, attitudes to work, etc.
ii. his personality – Form C of Cattell's 16PF (Cattell, Eber and Tatsuoka, 1970) was selected as a measure of personality because it affords a profile view (rather than concentrating on one highly specific dimension as some recent researchers prefer to do; Gemill and Heisler (1972) single out Machiavellianism and Caplan *et al.* (1975) Type A behaviour pattern, for example); is not overly-clinical for use with a sample of the general population; is well documented and validated and of proven reliability; it was able to serve a dual purpose by contributing a measure of psychological health in addition to a personality profile on 16 dimensions, and a British form is available. Form C was used which is self-administering and consists of 105 three-alternative choice items, comprising 16 scales. The following 16 source trait personality factors were used: factor A: reserved, detached, critical, aloof versus warm-hearted, outgoing, easygoing, participating; factor B: the less intelligent, concrete thinker versus more intelligent, abstract thinker; factor C: the higher ego strength versus emotional instability trait which is one of dynamic integration and maturity as opposed to uncontrolled, disorganised, general emotionality; factor E: the submissiveness versus dominance trait, which can be dichotomised as obedient, docile, accommodating as opposed to assertive, aggressive and competitive; factor F: the sober and serious personality versus the enthusiastic, happy-go-lucky one; factor G: the expedient who evades rules versus the conscientious rule-bound person; factor H: the shy, timid, threat-sensitive as opposed to the adventurous, socially bold personality; factor I: tough-minded versus tender-minded; factor L: 'trusting and free of jealousy' versus 'suspicious and hard to fool' trait; factor M: the conventional, practical and careful versus the imaginative, careless of practical matters person; factor N: the forthright, natural and sentimental versus the calculating, shrewd and penetrating; factor O: self-assured and con-

fident versus apprehensive and troubled; factor Q_1: reflects the continuum of conservatism to radicalism or from rigidity and upholding established ideas to experimenting and free thinking; factor Q_2: assesses the dichotomous trait of being group adherent at one end of the continuum to self-sufficient at the other; factor Q_3: low self-concept integration (undisciplined self-concept) to high self-concept control (following self-image); factor Q_4: relaxed and unfrustrated to high tension or frustrated and overwrought.

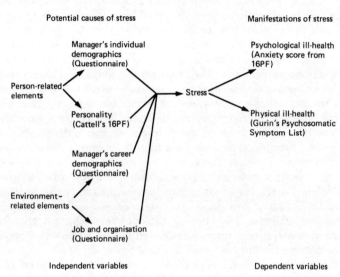

FIGURE 4.2 The P:E fit model operationalised

The job-related factors covered can similarly be classified under two headings:

i. 'career' demographics – job function, number of relocations, etc.
ii. job and organisational characteristics rated as being either sources of pressure or satisfaction or both by the managers. The Job and Organisational Characteristics Questionnaire, on which these replies were elicited (a full version of which is shown in the Appendix) was designed specifically for this study. It consists of a list of 61 potentially stressful job dimensions derived from the literature review and interviews and covers the six 'external' categories in Figure 4.1 above ('intrinsic to job', etc.). Respondents were asked to mark to what extent each factor applicable to them was a source

of pressure or satisfaction on a six-point scale (o to 5). Where appropriate they were allowed to indicate that it was *both* a pressure *and* a satisfaction by circling on both sides; many took the opportunity to do this. These 61 items were later reduced by factor analysis to 10 pressure and 8 satisfaction factors to simplify the manipulation of job-environment variables in subsequent regression analyses.

Turning to the right-hand side of Figure 4.2 we come up against the need to 'measure' stress. There is no one generally agreed way of doing this and the aspiring researcher meets problems at two levels. Firstly it is found that the direct referents of stress – chemical activity in the brain perhaps – are relatively inaccessible to study ('the experts' are not anyway agreed as to what these are) and one must depend on its outward manifestations as evidence. Having accepted that one must therefore measure its symptoms rather than stress itself, one finds that there is a wide range of available techniques but (again) no consensus as to which is or are 'the best', all having merits in particular circumstances. Symptoms can be looked for at three levels of the individual's functioning – the psychological, the physical and the behavioural – and can be approached via a continuum of reporting techniques, from the wholly objective (e.g. a measure of blood pressure) to the wholly subject-rated (often a check-list of symptoms supposed to have psychosomatic origins). Selection of the stress criterion measure to be included in a particular study is usually, as here, a matter of balancing conceptual and practical considerations; once the selection has been made however it is effectively 'the definition of stress' for that particular study.

In this study criteria manifestations of stress were measured at two levels: the psychological and the physical. Anxiety being the primary psychological symptom of stress, the 16PF second stratum factor of anxiety/adjustment (QII) was selected as a measure of emotional ill-health. Six of the 16PF scales make up the QII factor, they are C−, H−, L+, O−, Q3− and Q4+. This factor is reasonably reliable, has been extensively validated and has been used in other stress-related studies. Practical limitations meant that 'objective' physical stress data sources – medical records, physical examination, etc. – were not available. After some consideration and the piloting of two widely used symptom check-list type questionnaires it was decided to use the Gurin Psychosomatic Symptom List (Gurin, Veroff and Feld, 1960) as a criterion of physical health. On this scale the respondent is asked to mark the frequency (in this case during the last three months) of 24 symptoms of ill-health – sleeping difficulties, shortness of breath, upset stomach, etc. – which are widely agreed to be potentially stress-induced. This particular scale has the advantages over similar measures of being short, relatively non-clinical and of having a well-documented history of use in social science research (see Appendix for full version of this questionnaire).

In the results which follow qualitative and quantitative data are presented side-by-side. The emphasis is heavily toward the latter as it is the more substantive, the former being used more as a guide to interpretation.

THE SAMPLE

The sample were all senior male managers in a multinational company. Within this broad classification they were at times subdivided by job function – research, production, 'service', marketing and engineering or by managerial level – into 'lower', 'intermediate' and 'top' – for the purposes of analysis. The managers were an average age of 47; the majority married with growing families. Mobility is an inherent part of the company culture – 70% of respondents have been relocated, 40% three or more times and a quarter have worked abroad at some time – which proved a significant variable in analysis.

On the 16PF Personality scale the sample scored relatively high on the creativity-, self-sufficiency- and emotional stability-related factors. This was based on comparisons to the US Male Population norms (no British norms are yet available for this version of the test) and a large group of managers tested at the Administrative Staff College Henley (Hartston and Mottram, 1975). See Appendix for this data.

RESULTS

Results will be reported in two sections:

1. Job factors the managers themselves reported as being pressures or satisfactions, their replies to the Job and Organisational Characteristics Questionnaire.
2. Profiles of 'managers at risk' of showing symptoms of stress, described in person and environment terms.

SUBJECT-RATED JOB PRESSURES AND SATISFACTIONS

The Job and Organisational Characteristics Questionnaire offers two overlapping insights into managers' feelings about their jobs – first it tells us the relative importance of pressure and satisfaction for any particular aspect of their jobs. The sample's mean scores on pressure and satisfaction factors summarise this first viewpoint; these are shown in Table 4.1.

TABLE 4.1   Job factors derived from factor analysis: in descending order of magnitude

Pressures	Mean	Satisfactions	Description
	3.47	Relationships	Predominantly peer relationships.
	3.09	Recognition	Career success in terms of pay, promotion, responsibility, etc.
	2.58	Managing people	Relationships with subordinates.
Overload	1.76		Having more work than one can cope with.
	1.49	Challenging job	Job demands – especially those for time and activity.
Swamped in big company	1.19		Company's slowness in reacting to change, poor communications and conflict from implementing policies one doesn't agree with.
Job security	1.02		Fear of job loss.
Career development	0.65		Concern about promotion, pay and career prospects.
Uncertainty	0.45		Uncertainty and a lack of control over ones own life.
Lack of autonomy	0.45		Alienation and dissatisfaction with organisational role.
	0.43	Conflict	Striving against both colleagues and company – but from a secure position.
Underload	0.31		Thwarted ambition and work underload.
	0.31	Autonomy	Independence
	0.27	Faith in company	Trusts company and able to perform job easily.
Job challenges	0.16		Job demands – especially those on one's time and of dealing with people.
Relationships	0.11		Pressures from relationships with colleagues and subordinates.
	0.07	Belonging to large company	Security of large company membership.
No authority	0.18		Lack of responsibility and involvement.

In terms of relative intensity we find that satisfactions come significantly higher up the list than do pressures: managers whilst admitting job stressors are keen to make the point that they also enjoy their work. Relationships with both peers and subordinates ('Relationships' and 'Managing People' satisfactions respectively) make a substantial contribution to this. Success is also extremely important; career appears as a major consideration for this highly motivated sample: 'recognition' (satisfaction with past success) comes second on the positive side and concern about job security and career development third and fourth respectively on the negative side. The relative positions of these last two pressures was at first surprising in view of the calibre of the sample but it was felt that it reflects a reaction to the state of economic recession prevailing at the time of data collection rather than their true ordering of priorities. 'Overload' appears here and throughout the analyses as the greatest pressure the managers face; there is however a hint of ambiguity in this as several of the questionnaire items to which this factor refers appear again 'on the other side' as satisfaction of a 'challenging job'. The other pressures of note are those of 'working for a large company' and the 'uncertainty' and 'lack of autonomy' in which this can result.

Overlapping the above perspective it is important to note how pressure and satisfaction ratings combined for the original 61 questionnaire items; we find that the latter can be grouped under four headings. Whilst its content is consonant with that revealed in Table 4.1, Table 4.2

TABLE 4.2

Categorisation of job and organisational characteristics questionnaire items

---

  i. those reported mainly as satisfactions:
        communications,
        relationships.
  ii. those reported mainly as pressures:
        overload,
        ambiguity,
        career prospect worries,
        decisions,
        being in a large organisation.
 iii. those reported as pressures by some people and satisfactions by others:
        job security,
        having a taxing job,
        interpersonal conflict,
        time management.
 iv. those reported as both pressures and satisfactions by the same people:
        people–management,
        responsibility,
        challenging job.

---

makes an important structural contribution confirming the close association, shown here as interdependence, between stress and satisfaction. In so doing it provides research-generated support for the commonly held belief that over-zealous 'destressing' of the work environment would also remove much of the latter's satisfying challenge.

'STRESS VULNERABILITY PROFILES'

The above simple descriptions of managers' ratings realise only part of the potential of the results collected. The second stage in analysis was to pool all the person- and environment-related variables elicited and use multivariate statistical techniques to investigate their relationships with the dependent criteria of stress. A stepwise multiple regression sub-programme of the SPSS computer package (Nie, Bent and Hull, 1970) was used for this. Multiple regression relates independent and dependent variables in a manner which takes interactive effects into account. This statistical technique is a method of achieving the best linear prediction equation between a given set of independent variables and the dependent variable in question. Variables are incorporated in the equation in their order of significance thus allowing the researcher a margin of discretion as regards the choice of cut-off point. In this case the following criteria were used:

a. that the overall F for the equation was significant
b. that the partial regression coefficient for the individual independent variable being added was at a statistically significant or approaching significance level. Below this point not only is the coefficient insignificant but also the amount of variance contributed by each additional variable (R^2 change) is very small.

The regression equation thus obtained provides a profile painted in both job environment and person variable terms, of the manager 'at risk' of showing relatively high scores on the measures used; these will be referred to as 'stress vulnerability profiles'. The managers described are figments of the computer's imagination; they did not necessarily exist within the population studied each being the ultimate extrapolation of stress-prone trends. Multivariate techniques, whilst offering the researcher many benefits, are not without their drawbacks; it must particularly be remembered when reading the sections which follow that a correlation is a measure of association rather than of causation. Whilst the independent variables included here were chosen as being likely 'early contributors' to the stress sequence the possibility that significantly related factors may instead be subsidiary symptoms or consequences of stress must be borne in mind.

Throughout regression equations are derived for each of the two dependent variables separately. (As the anxiety score was calculated wholly from the first-stratum 16 PF factors the six of these which explained the greater part of variations in its score (88% in this case) were omitted from psychological ill-health analyses. These were 'affected by feelings' versus 'emotionally stable', 'shy' versus 'venturesome', 'trusting' versus 'suspicious', 'placid' versus 'apprehensive', 'undisciplined self-conflict' versus 'controlled' and 'relaxed' versus 'tense'.) The sample was first treated as a whole: these analyses were however relatively unsuccessful, the percentage variance in the dependent variable explained being disappointingly low – 24% for psychological and 33% for physical health respectively. It was therefore decided to carry out separate analyses for each job function and managerial level sub-group of the sample as systematic variations across the population were thought to be obscuring significant relationships. Analyses within sub-groups revealed profiles which were strikingly more significant and meaningful than those for the sample as a whole. The remainder of this section will therefore comprise three subsections:

A. analyses for the sample as a whole
B. analyses within job function subgroups
C. analyses within managerial level subgroups.

To ease the load on the reader the rather complex data has been simplified in three ways:

i. an assessment has been made as to whether the physical and psychological stress vulnerability profiles refer in fact to one and the same person; where it appears that they do one, amalgamated profile is presented. This assessment was based partly on the degree of association (measured by the Pearson correlation coefficient between the physical and psychological measures of stress; over the 18 profiles this varied from a non-significant 0.23 to a highly significant 0.67) and partly on the nature of the items making up the two profiles. For only four of the nine groupings considered are physical and psychological ill-health regressions presented separately.
ii. the following symbols are used in the multiple regression tables to distinguish types of independent variable and to indicate the direction of their relationship with the dependent variable:
S = satisfaction factor derived from factor analysis (i.e. subjects reported this job dimension as a source of satisfaction to them).
P = a pressure factor derived from factor analysis (reported by subjects as a source of pressure).
* = a factor from the 16PF Personality scale, scores toward the

quoted end of the bipolar scale were associated with higher stress scores.

$\uparrow$ = increasing values of the independent variable are associated with higher stress scores.

$\downarrow$ = decreasing values of the independent variable are associated with higher stress scores and

iii. insights from interview data have been used to round out the bare statistical results, the aim being to capture the gestalt of each profile rather than describe each equation in meticulous detail.

A. THE SAMPLE AS A WHOLE

For the sample as a whole, it is the manager with a 'calculating' personality profile, achieving lower scores on the intelligence scale and in a position characterised by overload and lack of autonomy who is 'at risk' of showing psychological stress symptoms. The four variables in Table 4.3 explain 24% of the anxiety score variance. The emergence of two 16PF dimensions (in view of the score's original derivation) shows that personality makes a substantial contribution to high anxiety. The 16PF intelligence scale (on which the sample as a whole scored significantly above the mean) consists of eight questions and is, therefore, too superficial to be treated too seriously. It did, however, appear consistently in association with higher stress scores and cannot be ignored; the phrase 'less bright' (rather than 'less intelligent') will be used to refer to lower scores on this dimension.

This description bears a close resemblance to that of the unhappy 'Machiavellian' personality described by Gemill and Heisler (1972) and there are striking hints in both sets of results of A-type characteristics (Friedman, 1969; Rosenman, Friedman and Strauss, 1964, 1966). The configuration is that of a striving individual who finds his (possibly unrealistic?) ambitions thwarted. Dissatisfaction with worker participation may then be a frustration even at senior managerial levels.

(The symbols used in Tables 4.3–4.20 represent the following:

1. Multiple R: shows how much correlation there is between the variables so far analysed and the factor to be explained.

2. R square: shows the amount of the variance contributed by the variables so far examined.

3. R square change: shows how much that particular variable contributes to predicting the anxiety or physical ill-health score.

The decimals can be regarded as percentage scores: so 0.328 can be seen as 32.8%, 0.451 as 45.1%. So in table 4:3 at Step 2 'Overload' and 'Shrewd' variables together correlate 0.402 with the anxiety score variance and contribute 0.162 to the variance of the anxiety score. 'Overload' on its own contributes 0.054.)

TABLE 4.3 Stepwise multiple regression analysis explanation of anxiety score variance for the sample as a whole (n = 179)

Step	Variable	Multiple R	R square	R square change
1	Shrewd*	0.328	0.107	0.107
2	↑ Overload P	0.402	0.162	0.054
3	Less intelligent*	0.451	0.204	0.042
4	↑ Lack of autonomy P	0.488	0.238	0.034
	Overall F = 12.785 p = 0.001			

TABLE 4.4 Stepwise multiple degression analysis explanation of physical ill-health score variance for the sample as a whole (n = 186)

Step	Variable	Multiple R	R square	R square change
1	Affected by feelings*	0.431	0.186	0.186
2	Tenderminded*	0.487	0.237	0.052
3	Tense*	0.538	0.290	0.052
4	Humble*	0.570	0.325	0.035
	Overall F = 20.787 p = 0.001			

Anxiety and physical ill-health scores for the sample as a whole correlated 0.47, p = 0.001.

The overall equation explaining physical ill-health bears out the dominant role of personality, four personality factors explaining 33% of the score variation to the total exclusion of job and organisational variables. Two of these factors ('affected by feelings' and 'tense') have already contributed significantly by definition to the calculation of the sample's anxiety scores; the fact that the remaining two ill-health predictors do not suggests that there is not a 100% overlap between our two criteria measures (and therefore between the individual's psychological and physical levels of functioning). Table 4.4 then, suggests a sensitive, neurotic personality type probably 'vulnerable' in a wide range of potentially stressful situations both in and outside work.

These sample-wide analyses whilst of interest at a general level are not strikingly convincing either statistically or descriptively and thus proved to be a further blow to any attempt to arrive at a concise list of actionable causes of stress. The sub-group analyses which follow achieve much higher levels of statistical prediction (although these must be treated with some caution as the samples were relatively small) and paint relatively full pictures of individuals 'at risk'.

B. JOB FUNCTION ANALYSES

i. *Managers in the research department*

The research manager 'at risk' of showing symptoms of stress is older
than others in his department but has less experience in terms of movement within the company. His personality profile is that of an assertive,
controlled, self-sufficient individual who is possibly less 'bright' than his
colleagues. He reports deriving satisfaction from managing people and
from working for the company but as these areas contribute to high
scores on the stress criteria measures we must conclude that he does not
find these particular aspects of his job easy; they are it seems in conflict
with his personality and (lack of) past experience. His diversion of time
and commitment to activities outside work (to which he looks for
satisfaction) is likely to put him under additional pressure. Smoking
(here a somewhat limited variable as it refers only to 'at work'
behaviour) is more probably a symptom than a cause of stress. Overall
this is the picture of a manager whose needs and abilities, whilst appropriate to his main function, do not match the demands (of managing
people and feeling at ease working in a large organisation) inherent
in his job – we might say that there is 'poor fit' between him and his
immediate environment. The personality profiles reported by Hartston
and Mottram (1975) suggest that this is a common risk for managers in
such functions. The results are also reminiscent of the introverted individual less able than his extrovert colleague to cope with interpersonal
problems described by Kahn *et al.* (1964).

Tables 4.5 and 4.6 show (respectively) the psychological and physical
health regression equations for managers in the research department.
Whilst correlation between the two stress scores was non-significant

TABLE 4.5   Explanation of anxiety for managers in research departments
(n = 28)

Step	Variable	Multiple R	R square	R square change
1	Assertive*	0.443	0.196	0.196
2	Toughminded*	0.596	0.355	0.159
3	↑ Managing People S	0.645	0.416	0.061
4	↓ No. of relocations	0.741	0.549	0.133
5	Smoking	0.774	0.599	0.050
6	Spending less time on work	0.800	0.640	0.041
7	Older	0.817	0.667	0.027
8	Self-sufficient*	0.838	0.701	0.035
	Overall F = 5.000 p = 0.033			

TABLE 4.6 Explanation of physical ill-health for managers in the research department (n = 29)

Step	Variable	Multiple R	R. square	R. square change
1	↑ Satisfaction outside work	0.435	0.190	0.190
2	↑ Managing people S	0.605	0.366	0.176
3	↑ Belonging to large company S	0.703	0.494	0.128
4	Less intelligent*	0.763	0.583	0.089
5	↓ No. of secondments	0.820	0.673	0.090
6	Self-sufficient*	0.867	0.752	0.079
7	Controlled*	0.906	0.821	0.069

Overall F = 11.808 p = 0.001

For research managers anxiety and physical ill-health correlate 0.23 (N.S.)

(r = 0.23), the two profiles show considerable overlap and so have been treated as one. (This suggests that for research managers a common cluster of causes leads to either psychological or physical stress effects, but not both – a possibility which will be given further consideration below.)

ii. *Managers on production sites*

The production manager works in a situation of constant demand. His job is both quantitatively and qualitatively overloading but typically he enjoys and derives direct and indirect satisfaction from mastering its challenges. The manager at risk is however not in the position to make the most of such opportunities for achievement as he is under additional pressure from two directions. Firstly there is the pressure from above, from geographically-distant, higher management who make decisions with which he may not agree but which he has to implement. (His doubts about his job security are a further indication of the poor quality of this relationship.) Secondly today's production manager feels his autonomy threatened from below. Greater participation for shop-floor and junior white collar workers is severely eroding his power and authority within the organisation. If we add in finally the personality dimensions predictive of psychological symptoms of stress – tendencies to be reserved and group-dependent – we see an individual who may well be reluctant to assert himself in this difficult situation.

Within the production function two distinctive 'stress profiles' were revealed; one, the more active pattern being associated with psychological symptoms of stress (Table 4.7) the other, a comparatively passive cluster with poorer scores on the physical health scale (Table 4.8).

Environmental variables dominate the explanation of high anxiety

TABLE 4.7   Explanation of anxiety for managers on production sites (n = 34)

Step	Variable	Multiple R	R square	R square change
1	↑ Job security P	0.472	0.222	0.222
2	↓ No. of secondments	0.613	0.375	0.153
3	↑ Overload P	0.685	0.469	0.093
4	Reserved•	0.741	0.549	0.081
5	↑ Belonging to large company S	0.801	0.642	0.092
6	↑ Challenging job S	0.855	0.730	0.089
7	↑ Lack of autonomy P	0.875	0.766	0.036
8	Group dependent•	0.893	0.800	0.032

Overall F = 11.890 p = 0.001

scores. Three themes emerge in the list of factors that the production manager 'at risk' reports as pressures:

1. a lack of job security
2. occuping an overloading and challenging job and
3. feelings of frustration at 'belonging to a large company' and the 'lack of autonomy' this involves.

In direct contrast the production manager at risk of showing *physical* symptoms of stress is not under obvious pressure from his current job. He is rather the victim of a lack of achievement in the past, being older but at a lower managerial level than his colleagues. His profile shows signs of emotional vulnerability (a tendency to worry); whether or not this has helped to cause his career frustration it is likely to make him react badly to 'failure'. The manager's wife is unlikely to work full-time which suggests that she too relies on his success for life satisfaction thus putting him under added pressure to achieve. The manager in this situation may well find accepting and adjusting to having reached his career ceiling difficult especially if he feels that he must hide his disappointment from his wife. The appearance of 'non-smoking' as a factor associated with higher stress scores is somewhat difficult to explain – perhaps it is those managers who do not have some tension-release mechanism (or whose personality type makes doing so less likely) who are the more 'at risk'.

As for the research manager, the production manager's psychological and physical stress criteria scores are not significantly related (for all remaining analyses correlations between the two scores are statistically significant). This suggests that managers in these two groups tend to separate their physical and psychological modes of functioning. They may therefore appear less susceptible to stress than their colleagues as they do not reveal symptoms at a certain level (in the showing of emotions perhaps) whilst in reality they are reacting more covertly. Such segregation (however it has come about developmentally) may help to explain why some people seem able to 'soldier on', despite massive disabilities, whilst others find that even a minor lapse in health 'permeates' all other areas of their life space.

TABLE 4.8   Explanation of physical ill-health for managers on production sites (n = 36)

Step	Variable	Multiple R	R square	R square change
1	Affected by feelings*	0.510	0.260	0.260
2	Humble*	0.609	0.371	0.110
3	Lower managerial level	0.608	0.463	0.091
4	Older	0.751	0.563	0.100
5	Non-smoking	0.781	0.609	0.046
6	Wife less likely to work	0.817	0.668	0.059
7	Less intelligent*	0.840	0.706	0.037

Overall F = 8.557 p = 0.001

For production managers anxiety and physical ill-health correlate 0.32 (N.S.)

iii. *Managers in service departments*

It was a particular relationship to the rest of the organisation rather than job content that members of the service group had in common – it is not surprising therefore that immediate job elements fail to appear in the profiles of managers 'at risk'. It is their position in the organisation which is more a cause for concern to this function, the environmental factors associated with stress all reflecting feelings of a lack of autonomy and authority.

TABLE 4.9   Explanation of anxiety for managers in service departments (n = 36)

Step	Variable	Multiple R	R square	R square change
1	Shrewd*	0.474	0.225	0.225
2	↑ Lack of autonomy P	0.591	0.349	0.124
3	↑ Time since last relocation	0.652	0.425	0.076
4	↓ Time since last promotion	0.740	0.548	0.123
5	↑ Belonging to large company S	0.770	0.594	0.046

Overall F = 7.593 p = 0.001

TABLE 4.10   Explanation of physical ill-health for managers in service departments (n = 37)

Step	Variable	Multiple R	R square	R square change
1	Tense•	0.561	0.315	0.315
2	↓ Autonomy S	0.707	0.499	0.184
3	Humble•	0.758	0.574	0.075
4	Affected by feelings	0.790	0.624	0.050
5	Wife less likely to work	0.818	0.668	0.044
6	↓ No authority P	0.848	0.719	0.051

Overall F = 10.667 p = 0.001

For service managers anxiety and physical ill-health correlate 0.67 p = 0.001

It would seem that, for the manager 'at risk', the service role of having expert knowledge but being in an advisory rather than a directly participating position when decisions are being made is a source of frustration. Viewed in the context of the personality characteristics which contribute to higher stress scores – a tendency to anxiety twinned with ambition – the problem his organisational role presents is even more readily understandable. Again it would appear that the manager's wife is likely to be at least financially, if not emotionally, dependent on his career success – another incentive/pressure for him to do well. Having been recently promoted has not served to improve his feelings of independence (interview replies showed that it is a mistake to think that top management have boundless power); in fact it would appear that becoming more involved in (and dependent on) the company has served to accentuate this employee's feelings of powerlessness. In both its person and environment components this profile bears a striking resemblance to that of the dissatisfied Machiavellian manager described by Gemill and Heisler (1972) and referred to above. It suggests that ambition and a high need for independence are 'dangerous' characteristics for the service manager in a large company especially if he is by nature prone to anxiety.

iv. *Managers in the marketing and sales department*

The marketing manager at risk is very similar in character to his service department colleague – he too shows considerable evidence of being anxiety prone combining this with ambition; his job situation is however markedly different. For him the main problem is work overload and he reports both too much to do and too many challenges in his job. French and Caplan (1973) distinguish these as quantitative and qualitative overload respectively. As with the researcher there is a

suggestion that looking outside work for satisfaction may be reducing
the manager's ability to cope with what seems to be a highly demanding
position. This is possibly the profile of an individual who has been over-
promoted (or has, because he is ambitious, allowed himself to be) for
there is no evidence (as there was for the service manager) that his job
demands have recently peaked. Again it appears to be the non-smoking
manager who is the more vulnerable.

TABLE 4.11   Explanation of anxiety for managers in marketing departments
(n = 62)

Step	Variable	Multiple R	R square	R square change
1	Shrewd*	0.400	0.159	0.159
2	↑ Overload P	0.526	0.277	0.118
3	↑ Time since last relocation	0.580	0.336	0.059
4	Non-smoker	0.631	0.400	0.062
5	Reserved*	0.649	0.420	0.023
6	↑ Job challenges P	0.670	0.449	0.028

Overall F = 6.93 p = 0.001

TABLE 4.12   Explanation of physical ill-health for managers in marketing
departments (n = 64)

Step	Variable	Multiple R	R square	R square change
1	Affected by feelings*	0.485	0.235	0.235
2	Tenderminded*	0.573	0.328	0.093
3	Tense*	0.626	0.392	0.064
4	↑ Satisfaction outside work	0.660	0.436	0.044
5	↓ Challenging job P	0.686	0.471	0.035

Overall F = 9.263 p = 0.001
For marketing managers anxiety and physical ill-health correlate 0.56, p = 0.001

With the same vulnerable personality profile the last two manager
groups nevertheless find themselves in objectively very different but, in
terms of their resulting experiences of stress, very similar situations. The
first, the service manager, has chosen a combination of speciality and
size of company in which his needs are unlikely to be met. The second,
the marketing manager, has let his needs outrun his capabilities to such
an extent that he is in danger.

v. *Managers in the engineering department*

TABLE 4.13   Explanation of anxiety for managers in engineering departments
(n = 19)

Step	Variable	Multiple R	R square	R square change
1	Less intelligent*	0.524	0.274	0.274
2	Older	0.696	0.485	0.211
3	Lower managerial level	0.771	0.594	0.109
4	↑ Lack of autonomy P	0.829	0.687	0.093
5	↑ Challenging job S	0.866	0.750	0.063
6	↑ Satisfaction outside work	0.930	0.865	0.115

Overall F = 12.765 p = 0.001

TABLE 4.14   Explanation of physical ill-health for managers in engineering
departments (n = 20)

Step	Variable	Multiple R	R Square	R square change
1	↑ Challenging job S	0.626	0.392	0.392
2	Apprehensive*	0.733	0.537	0.145
3	Practical*	0.834	0.680	0.143
4	Undisciplined self-conflict*	0.858	0.736	0.056
5	↑ Job security P	0.877	0.770	0.034
6	Tenderminded*	0.912	0.832	0.052

Overall F = 9.875 p = 0.001

For engineering managers anxiety and physical ill-health correlate 0.65,
p = 0.003

The most surprising characteristic of this last job function stress
profile, is the prominence of reported satisfaction from job challenges.
It is only when we view this element in the context of the remaining job
factor pattern that this becomes understandable. The engineer at risk
shows several symptoms of being dissatisfied with his career progress: he
is older but at a lower managerial level than his colleagues in the department, feels that he lacks autonomy and is also unsure about his future
job security. This pattern of concerns implies that he does not have the
power and authority to perform as he would like irrespective of the opportunities he feels there are for achievement. His personality profile
suggests that he is unlikely to cope easily with such a situation of
perceived external constraint, he is practical but sensitive and worrying.
This manager too looks outside work for satisfaction but, in his case, it

is likely to be an attempt to compensate for reduced job involvement rather than a competitive drain on his energies. Several factors may be at work here. This profile more than any other suggests a group whose situation has been worsened (perhaps largely caused) by the economic climate at the time of data collection (mid-1970s). Engineering departments within companies can only exist if they are backed financially, and are amongst the first to suffer from cutbacks in capital expenditure during a recession. The feeling of being undervalued which permeates this profile however also echoes the longer-term concerns of Davis (1975) when he described the 'muddy image' of this profession in Britain especially when compared to its high status abroad.

C. MANAGERIAL LEVEL ANALYSES

An alternative way of subdividing the sample is by managerial level. This segmenting variables revealed regression equations of lower predictive power than those for job function but which are nonetheless of interest. Not surprisingly, in view of their derivation, career development themes dominate the profiles. (It is important to note in passing that for this sample managerial level and age were not significantly statistically related – i.e. promotion is not an automatic right of seniority).

i. *Lower management*

The two profiles of the lower manager 'at risk' are closely similar to those of the sample as a whole. The same four personality factors dominate the equation for poor physical health but are joined by 'practical' to achieve a much higher predictive power of 54%.
The manager at risk of showing symptoms of psychological ill-health is again the 'ambitious', 'less bright' personality type in a 'work overload' situation but this time it would appear that he is also taxed by interpersonal conflict (a job element he reports enjoying). His conservative

TABLE 4.15   Explanation of anxiety for lower management (n = 90)

Step	Variable	Multiple R	R square	R square change
1	Shrewd*	0.398	0.158	0.158
2	↑ Overload P	0.450	0.203	0.045
3	Conservative*	0.490	0.240	0.037
4	Less intelligent*	0.526	0.277	0.037
5	↑ Conflict S	0.558	0.312	0.035
	Overall F = 7.069 p = 0.001			

TABLE 4.16 Explanation of physical ill-health for lower management (n = 91)

Step	Variable	Multiple R	R square	R square change
1	Affected by feelings*	0.463	0.214	0.214
2	Tenderminded*	0.567	0.321	0.107
3	Tense*	0.636	0.405	0.084
4	Humble*	0.689	0.474	0.070
5	Practical*	0.735	0.540	0.065

Overall F = 18.300 p = 0.001
For lower managers anxiety and physical ill-health correlate 0.53, p = 0.001

tendencies help perhaps to explain the apparent contradiction in this last association.

As these profiles are already familiar, and the latter equation achieves a relatively poor explanation of the stress score variance (only 31%) no attempt will be made to elaborate their descriptions here.

ii. *Intermediate management*

In the profiles of intermediate managers 'at risk' we find the oft repeated 'sensitive' (for physical ill-health) and 'ambitious' (for anxiety) vulnerable persnality patterns heavily overlaid with contributing job factor stressors. This lends credence to the claim made elsewhere (e.g. Kay, 1974) that positions at this organisational level are intrinsically stressful. Whilst these two profiles are rather different in detail they show a common theme.

Dissatisfaction with workload makes a substantial contribution to the explanation of psychological ill-health; the fact that both underload and overload are associated with higher stress scores suggests that a cur-

TABLE 4.17 Explanation of anxiety for intermediate management (n = 66)

Step	Variable	Multiple R	R square	R square change
1	Shrewd*	0.273	0.075	0.075
2	↑ Overload P	0.365	0.133	0.059
3	↑ Underload P	0.454	0.206	0.073
4	↓ Conflict S	0.526	0.276	0.070
5	Less intelligent*	0.575	0.330	0.054
6	↑ Job challenges P	0.603	0.363	0.033

Overall F = 5.23, p = 0.001

vilinear relationship is involved. Deriving decreasing satisfaction from conflict, the competition which for many is the main stimulus to progress, and feeling unable to cope with the challenges one's job offers are also associated with vulnerability. This is the profile of a manager who, whilst still ambitious, appears to have run out of the energy necessary to push himself both in his current position and towards future success.

TABLE 4.18 Explanation of physical ill-health for intermediate management (n = 69)

Step	Variable	Multipe R	R square	R square change
1	Apprehensive*	0.475	0.225	0.225
2	↑ Lack of autonomy P	0.552	0.305	0.079
3	↓ Faith in company S	0.592	0.350	0.045
4	↓ Uncertainty P	0.635	0.403	0.052
5	Tenderminded*	0.662	0.438	0.035
6	↑ Career development	0.687	0.473	0.034

Overall F = 8.364, p = 0.001

For intermediate managers anxiety and physical ill-health correlate 0.43, p = 0.001

The poor physical health equation reveals similar themes but possibly at a later stage when the manager's career progress has in fact been affected. This manager 'at risk' feels that he lacks authority and is concerned about his career future. His reports of less pressure from uncertainty summarise this – whilst uncertainty can be a source of stress it is also an important stimulus to growth and achievement; its presence indicates challenge, hope and future prospects. This manager's declining faith in the company is further confirmation of 'career ceiling' and demoralisation.

iii. *Top management*

The top manager 'vulnerable to stress' is still relatively young but appears to have come to a career standstill. His profile suggests considerable past success but he is dissatisfied with the position he has achieved. He likes conflict, a sign that he has retained his driving competitive spirit, but does not (partly as a result?) enjoy work relationships which is the most important job dimension for managers at his level. There are signs that he is becoming dissatisfied with the company, not because he lacks faith in it (quite the reverse), but because he feels swamped by its size. This is the profile of the high-flier who has reached his peak too early and appears to have had a false impression of what

TABLE 4.19 Explanation of anxiety for top management (n = 23)

Step	Variable	Multiple R	R square	R square change
1	↑ Time since last relocation	0.683	0.466	0.466
2	↓ Relationships S	0.823	0.677	0.211
3	Smoking	0.903	0.815	0.138
4	↑ Career development P	0.932	0.869	0.054
5	↑ Swamped in big company P	0.967	0.935	0.066

Overall F = 46.045 p = 0.001

TABLE 4.20 Explanation of physical ill-health for top management (n = 25)

Step	Variable	Multiple R	R square	R square change
1	Affected by feelings•	0.469	0.220	0.220
2	↑ Faith in company S	0.594	0.353	0.133
3	Suspicious•	0.721	0.519	0.166
4	↑ Conflict S	0.801	0.641	0.122
5	↓ Belonging to large company S	0.859	0.738	0.097
6	↑ Time since last promotion	0.946	0.894	0.056
7	Younger	0.974	0.948	0.054
8	↑ No. of relocations	0.989	0.979	0.031

Overall F = 74.658 p = 0.001
For top managers anxiety and physical ill-health correlate 0.44, p = 0.04

'life at the top' would be like. In interviews several top managers expressed such disappointment and frustration; they felt that they had less authority and independence and had to rely more on the uncertain use of power and influence than at more satisfying, lower organisational levels.

Again a career development explanation fits the data. The two equations although elaborated *via* different elements show considerable common ground.

These managerial level analyses are also of interest viewed in series. Looking back we find many similarities between levels but also subtle differences which deserve comment. Overlapping the typical vulnerable, 'affected by feelings' personality pattern there are for example variations in secondary characteristics: *lower and intermediate managers* 'at risk' share a 'calculating' outlook and 'lower intelligence' scale scores; the former also show conventional leanings and the latter a dominant 'apprehensive' trait: *top managers* are 'independent' and 'conscientious'. The job demands that appear as stressors also change with level: *intermediate* positions are characterised by a wide range of pressing environmental demands, whilst *top* managers are required to adopt a qualitatively different approach to their work in order to succeed. Whilst it is those who cannot cope at a particular level and are therefore unlikely to go further in the organisation who are most vulnerable to stress, survival through one level does not guarantee that one will be able to avoid stress at the next.

SUMMARY AND SOME IMPLICATIONS

Rather than reveal simple answers, the analyses served to elucidate some of the intricacies, both practical and conceptual, of this highly complex topic. We see from the regression analyses that whilst the universe of potential stressors is vast, for any group of individuals with common characteristics it can be reduced to a manageable number of critical dimensions. The 'stress vulnerability profiles' thus generated have considerable practical value. They give us insight into the job experiences of sub-groups within the organisational population and could act as a basis for change policies should any group be identified as relatively highly stressed. They could also be used, with some caution, as an additional guide in selection and recommendation for training. In addition we find five themes which are repeated often enough in the stress-explanatory equations to suggest that they may repay company-wide consideration. Two of these are person-related – being *anxiety-prone* and *ambitious* – and three job–environment–related – *work overload, lack of autonomy* and *concern about career development*. What actions are practicable and desirable to reduce the potential ill-effects of any pressures identified as being generally applicable should ideally be worked out between managers and higher (policy-forming) management in a given company and will depend as much on the norms and values prevailing in that company culture as on the presenting problem. Paying attention to them need not (indeed should not) be a threatening discontinuity in the organisation's current activities – the minimisation of harmful stress is already the covert aim of much training, personnel work, organisational change, etc. and analysis such as the above simply provides detailed, company-specific data to guide in their development.

The practical value of such data is relatively obvious; it is probably more important here to emphasise its structural, more generalisable implications. We find substantial evidence to support the P:E fit model of stress causation already favoured by the more innovative theorists (e.g. Lazarus, 1971; McLean, 1976). 1976). 15 of the 18 regression equations include P and E variables in interaction in order to achieve an adequate explanation of stress score variance. In addition we find no list of generally applicable causes of stress. The diversity of respondents' initial replies to the Job and Organisational Characteristics Questionnaire shows the individuality of stress-definition clearly; regression analyses support it with their failure to achieve conceptual or statistical significance until focused on relatively small, but meaningful, population sub-groups and their almost complete lack of duplication over the sixteen sub-group profiles. Adding these two findings together we must conclude that stress is the outcome of the interaction of a particular individual with a particular environment at a particular point in time. It is therefore unlikely to be easily foreseen or prevented and must be coped with at this *ad hoc* level; we must develop flexible strategies to catch the manager as he 'falls' rather than prevent him climbing. Elsewhere we have explored ways in which this might be achieved (Marshall, 1977; Cooper and Marshall, 1976) emphasising that stress should be managed rather than removed, that its control is a joint responsibility of the employing company and the manager concerned and concluding:

> 'Two basic needs, therefore, emerge – the first is for an organisational atmosphere and structure in which the employee feels he is free to express his inability to cope, discuss his fears and ask for help; the second is for an individual who is aware of his needs to do these things and able to communicate meaningfully'. (Cooper and Marshall, 1976).

The greater significance of sub-group than sample-wide analyses also has methodological implications: both academic and organisation-based researchers must recognise the presence of significant sub-groups within the populations studied to be meaningful and writers who talk of 'managers' as a homogeneous group should be treated with extreme caution.

The role of satisfaction in 'the stress equation' is revealed as being highly significant but requires further exploration to be fully understood. In future research both pressure and satisfaction need therefore to be taken into account in order to achieve a comprehensive view of the individual's work experience. It would also appear that increasing satisfaction (as well as obviously pressure) contributes to higher stress scores – i.e. that people enjoy things which viewed objectively aren't really 'good' for them. This is perhaps everyday common knowledge but is not always appreciated in academic studies; it should caution further researchers against taking too narrow a view of the stress area.

The results reported here and the further thought about 'stress research' they stimulate serve to widen rather than narrow down the range of applicability of 'stress research' and lead one easily to the conclusion of Wolff (1968):

'Since stress is a dynamic state within an organism in response to a demand for adaptation, and since life itself entails constant adaptation, living creatures are continually in a state of more or less stress'.

It is not intended by this suggestion to dismiss stress as too broad a topic to study, the potential benefits of understanding are greatly increased by the widening of its definition; unfortunately so are the methodological and conceptual difficulties of research.

5 What Managers and their Wives say about Stress at Work: In-depth Interviews

A second and very important phase of our research was a series of in-depth interviews with a sample of the managers and their wives in order to obtain more qualitative and personal information on managerial stressors and their consequences.

From the interview transcripts of 35 senior managers and 28 of their wives (those of lower levels and some which dealt almost solely with managerial relocation were not considered), 35 manager 'profiles' were derived for analysis. The seven broad categories of potential stressors – 'job', 'role', 'relationships', etc. (used in the literature review) – were taken as main headings to classify the job pressures and satisfactions mentioned by interviewees. Sub-categories were evolved and developed during analysis. This approach is consistent with the principles outlined by Glaser and Strauss (1967) for the generation of substantive theory by comparative analysis. In practice for example the overlap between two main categories – 'Role in Organisation' and 'Organisational Structure and Climate' – was so great that these were amalgamated and appear as 'Role Pressures in a Large Organisation'. As an estimate of the relative importance of the different issues, the percentage of profiles for which a particular comment was made is frequently reported in brackets in the text. It was decided to take the more conservative course by scoring reported rather than inferred causes, the percentages are therefore considerably underestimated but have some relative validity. We find that interviewees varied widely in the terms they used to describe their jobs; whilst there is general *agreement* on only certain issues there is substantial *consensus*. This individuality of expression has for the most part been preserved to give a richer picture.

The emphasis in this analysis was towards the *pressure* rather than the *satisfaction* side of the manager's jobs (the former being the main theme of research) and managers elaborated their replies more on this dimension. To temper this negative bias it should be remembered (from the empirical findings) that managers also derive considerable satisfaction from their work.

Sections 1 to 7 below describe in detail the job pressures mentioned by interviewees; in sections 8 and 9 job satisfactions and coping techniques (respectively) are reported more briefly and section 10 summarises these qualitative findings.

The job pressures reported by the sample fall into 6 main categories:

PRESSURES INTRINSIC TO THE JOB

In the literature review in Chapter 3 it was suggested that particular occupational groups would be subject to their own distinct 'stress profiles'; this appears to be so. Two such patterns will be described here as examples:

A. JOB FUNCTION

One interesting group of service managers to examine are the managers in the patent department. They tend to be 'doers' rather than man-managers. Each has his own area of responsibility and handles patents applications and defences for products in that area. The work involves detailed knowledge of legal and constantly changing technical matters, is controlled by deadlines and mistakes could cost the company thousands if not millions of pounds. All interviewees found the time pressures and the fact that they could 'never let up' stressful and reported being overloaded. Other pressures were the need to always be right, boring repetition, the frustration of situations in which there was no straightforward answer, problems of communications with other departments, having 'to rely on other people to do their bit' and the occasional necessity to make judgements on inadequateeate information. It appeared that all patents personnel felt this 'pressure of work' and that as a result there was little time during the day for informal interaction in this department. All however derived some satisfaction from their jobs – from the constant variety of content and the challenges it offered – and several said that experience of 'having coped in the past' made them less worried than they used to be.

Managers in patents also reported particularly acute career development worries – professional qualification is *via* a series of stringent exams; once this is achieved however no further growth is required or possible without moving out of the department (an unlikely course were it to receive official sanction since it would mean starting again from scratch). Career prospects outside the company were also seen by the sample as being severely restricted as they necessitated working in London, required generalised rather than the specialised experience possessed, and other jobs were comparatively poorly paid. The feeling of being in a 'dead-end job' soured job satisfaction and accentuated job pressures for managers in this department – for some the future appeared to be 30 years of being 'stuck in the same groove'.

Elements of this profile are apposite to other function groups. For example:

time pressures, deadlines and restricted opportunities outside because of within-company experience were reported by *accountants*,

problems of communication with other departments by those who work with *computers* and

problems of getting enough information on which to plan and make decisions and having to deal with routine matters by other individual managers in various departments.

Pressures involved in the second profile – that for *production managers* – are in contrast peculiar to this function. Industrial relations problems are a major cause of pressure for this group (26%) but when resolved act as a major source of satisfaction. Several managers (80%) were concerned that too much attention was paid to these aspects and not enough to 'the real work' of producing. A few managers expressed frustration at having to attend so much to 'trivial emotional problems', having only talk as a persuasive weapon, having to resolve disputes through organisations rather than known personnel and the 'knowledge' that in all exchanges their subordinates have the 'upper hand'.

Production problems and the possibilities of an accident (both for the injury involved and the black mark it represents) were also mentioned as worries. Although one is 'fighting on *different* fronts all the time', production is a constant demand situation (8.5%). Working at a production unit involves spending more time at work compared with being at Head Office and managers are often on call. Several wives complained about the uncertainties of this type of situation (18%) and of disrupted social and holiday plans but many husbands appear to enjoy, or to have enjoyed, it especially in the early 'start-up' days – 'the excitement, it just takes you'. Even the crisis situation of a strike in which a manager had been helping to run the plant as well as do his own job was remembered by his wife rather than him as stressful.

Other functions were not covered so intensively in interviews and no full profiles can be described from the data – initial elements are however apparent: for example the *personnel officer* who lacks direct authority, attends to a wide range of diverse duties, cannot see when he has made progress, has allegiance to no particular group but feels that he must be 'acceptable' to everyone (8.5%).

B. WORKLOAD

Of the 35 managers whose profiles were scored in detail only 11% did not complain of work overload (and of these 8.5% had come to a disappointing career 'standstill'). The remaining managers (89%) all reported that they had more work than they could cope with. From overall replies and expressions of work stress a subjective assessment of each manager's handling of his workload was made: 42% appeared to be able to 'contain' this overload – i.e. give as much as they wanted to the job (in some cases this was a lot). 29% to be overpowered by job demands through little fault of their own and 29% to be overloaded for a combination of job and 'personality reasons'.

Heavy workload is therefore a characteristic of jobs at this managerial level, but some jobs are more controllable than others and some individuals are better able to handle this than their colleagues. 13% of the managers thought that they were particularly overloaded in their jobs compared to others in similar positions; for various reasons they reported that they were in effect 'doing two jobs' but that this was not appreciated by the company. 6% said that they were not prepared to point this out as they did not want 'to ask for charity' and doubted whether they would be 'understood' as 'everyone else is under stress too'.

As one would expect in this situation, time pressures (23%) – 'everything wanted by yesterday', 'no time to sit and think' – and a sense of urgency – 'you can never let up' – were widely reported. Spending lots of time in meetings (14%) bureaucratic paperwork (6%) and loss of precious work time due to travelling (11%) were seen as further aggravations.

C. PEOPLE–MANAGEMENT

People–management in general (as opposed to site-specific industrial relations problems) was a further pressure reported throughout the sample. Delegating was the main cause for concern here (20%): learning how to delegate, adapting to managing rather than doing (resisting the temptation of getting involved in the detail oneself) and taking on work oneself because of a subordinate's perceived incompetence. At times of economic crisis responsibility for people can be an added worry. Several interviewees (14%) reported the depressive effects of having to make employees redundant during the country's last economic downturn. The trauma of this memory was heightened for some by fears they had about their own job security, the still evident poor morale of survivors and the suspicion that is might happen again.

D. PRESSURES WHICH INCREASE WITH MANAGERIAL LEVEL

Certain pressures appear to be particularly related to achieving higher managerial levels. The move from being the man in charge of a unit ('the job, I enjoyed most in my whole career'), to less autonomy at a higher level was the most frustrating and surprising of these (14%). At these levels 'doing' is unimportant and new skills are required as 'persuading' becomes the main medium of achievement (31%); annual review meetings were mentioned as particularly stressful events (8.5%). Responsibility is however as great or greater than it was when one-man decisions were admissable – never being able to escape from responsibility, the need to get important decisions right and to keep pace with and answer questions about what is going on were also stresses for managers at this level. For some the job becomes so big that it stops being enjoyable – but there are few opportunities for going back 'honourably'.

E. EXTRA-COMPANY FORCES

Circumstances outside the company can also act as job pressures for different groups. The economic situation and legislation have for example put added demands on accountancy departments; the former has also encouraged non-recruitment policies which means that the organisation cannot expand accordingly. Managers on production sites are also 'under fire' at the moment; besides coping with shortages and pressure from 'choosey' customers they must sustain workforce morale in readiness for the anticipated upturn.

The rapidity of change was also a concern to many managers (23%) – in general, as the company tries to keep up, and at a personal level as they try to keep pace with changing technologies and professional practices. Change within the organisation can also have effects and 8.5% of the managers reported stressful periods in which they had had to adapt to the dictates of a new higher management regime.

ROLE PRESSURES IN A LARGE ORGANISATION

The second main 'constellation' of pressures are those associated with the manager's role in the organisation. On examination most of those reported by the sample are consequences of working for a large rather than a small organisation.

Managers felt that large company membership restricted their autonomy; many would like to make more decisions on their own without having to co-ordinate with other units of the company, to be able to recruit without going to the board, to have more say and greater budgetary control. Having the expertise but not the official authority to influence decisions in a particular area was a similar complaint (8.5%). The sample showed their frustration in a variety of ways: feeling trapped, stifled, like a 'small cog in a big machine', pressured from having so many bosses, 'you lose sight of the outside world' and expressing disappointment at the relatively low-status job title for the work done.

A further difficulty is that of passing on orders or implementing policies (for the most part personnel) with which one does not agree. Some managers felt that having been allowed to express their opinions they had been treated fairly and it was acceptable if those responsible for the outcome made the decision, a couple of managers however reported long, tiring battles after which higher management had at last been made 'to see sense'. It is conflict such as this which results in the manager feeling that he is 'caught between two camps'. The greatest frustration over such issues was expressed by two managers who said that it was often difficult to discover on what reasoning the ('unreasonable') decision had been based, and another who felt that changes often followed fashion rather than commonsense. Whilst these are 'only' the possibly mistaken perceptions of a few individuals they are nonetheless real to those concerned.

'Poor communications' may well contribute to the pressures described so far in this section and one manager felt that matters could be greatly improved if the company would learn what to communicate 'consultatively' and what to command; on issues where there is effectively no choice he felt that it was unsettling if the former approach was adopted.

The above criticisms are more those aimed at large company membership *per se* than at this specific firm which was highly praised by both managers and their wives for the care it took of its employees. Whilst the company has in fact been quick to adopt participative management practices in many areas these findings do suggest that this has not been completely successful and particularly that participation at one level can be a source of stress for that level's superiors.

Another facet of working for a large company, which frequently translated into a pressure, was 'uncertainty about ones future' and part of the informal communications within the company was what might be termed the 'with this company you can never tell' myth. You can never tell particularly when you will be asked to move to a new job although several interviewees (especially wives) thought that it was more likely to be when you had just bought a new house, your wife was pregnant or an extensive foreign business trip was planned!

PRESSURE FROM RELATIONSHIPS

Relationship problems played little part in the interviewees' reports of job stress. Situations in which they had caused or were causing pressure were:

'personality clashes' (20%)

having been promoted into an awkward situation (11%) (e.g. over someone else's head)

moving to a 'bad atmosphere' (6%)

liaising with other departments (6%)

feeling watched by one's predecessor (6%)

having given one's superior the wrong impression and needing to correct this (3%) and

having made changes and built-up resentment (3%)
Lack of relationships at 'lonelier' higher management levels (11%) especially in terms of not being able to 'cry on anyone else's shoulder' (11%) was also reported as a cause of stress.

CAREER DEVELOPMENT AND JOB SECURITY PRESSURES

Concern about career development and job security is the fourth main category of pressures. The sample was drawn from a highly successful population; within it however different degrees of success were evident and these were reflected in different degrees of satisfaction with career progress. Looking at the overall interview profiles the following subjective classifications were arrived at by the researcher:

young frustrated managers	6%
progressing gradually (but not confident about next step)	40%
confidently 'on the way up'	14%
reached career ceiling – but satisfied	14%
reached career ceiling – frustrated	17%
demoted – satisfied	3%
demoted – frustrated	6%

Only 31% of managers had no career problems at the time of contact; for the remainder 'career development' was mixed with 'job security' worries.

Complete lack of career prospects has been described above as being almost inevitable for those in the patents department; this is however an atypically objective cause of pressure – feeling that one was wasting one's time, being in a job for three or four years, feeling completely on top of the job, underestimated, bored, stale or feeling one has reached a 'dead end', seeing others come and go and subordinates promoted above you were all mentioned as signs that promotion was, or had been, overdue (54%). Most interviewees had acquired an expectation of a 'normative rate' of progress and could discuss times at which they had 'fallen behind' in this way. Managers had adopted various strategies for righting this situation; the most popular was to look outside the company for work and 23% of those interviewed had at some time done this (one felt that 'those who get on, get out'). Others had tried working hard, accepting any new job solely 'to get out', 'persuasion' and concentrating on the 'visible' aspects of their jobs.

Whilst luck and opportunity were considered to be the most important fate-determining factors (6%) many of those who felt that their progress had at some time been retarded could quote what they felt to be contributory causes:

being too blunt and outspoken

failing to pass essential exams due to lack of training and experience in a 'backwater'

having joined the company 'late' (i.e. not immediately after graduating) and

having failed to accept a previously offered move/promotion.

The latter reason was the most frequently mentioned and many managers and their wives were of the opinion that a refusal to move meant future restriction of opportunities (a widely held company myth). For this reason, as well as the challenge involved in a new job and the desire not to block other people's progress, most found it impossible to refuse promotion.

Viewed in the long-term most managers subscribed to the belief expressed by some, that theirs was a 'young man's game' (11%). One has to fight hard when young and reassess the situation at about 40 years of age ('I'll sacrifice family life for work until then'). Several managers reported accepting promotion before they felt fully able to cope with their previous job suggesting that 'over promotion' is a real danger at this career phase.

In middle-age new factors must be considered; there was no consensus as to how 'job importance' changes with age or life stage though most interviewees agree that it did. Some factors act to restrict ambition: the decreased monetary incentive of promotion (due to the tax man) (14%), fears of technical obsolescence in areas outside ones immediate concern (8.5%), a need for security (3%), an awareness of the psychological costs of increased responsibility (3%) and the growing importance of other life areas (partly as a result of interpersonal training courses) (3%) all reduce the urge to push ahead no matter what. Interviewees said that they could 'be more choosey'. Other factors can act to redress the balance and increase job involvement: as promotion means that the job takes up more time (8.5%) and gives greater satisfaction (6%), as more money compensates for the inconveniences (3%), as the family grows up and leaves (3%) and heavier financial commitments necessitate further salary increases (3%). For many this is a time of reassessment especially in view of the restricted number of places available at higher organisational levels. Managers at this stage felt that opportunities were further restricted by the increasingly rapid rise of younger managers and slowed company expansion over the last few years and predicted that early retirement would become commonplace in the near future. It is the exceptional older manager who feels that he has good prospects outside the company (one, who had had unusually extensive early experience outside) and it is 'easy' to wonder if one would have fared better elsewhere (3%) and to resent the 'fact' that one has no choice but stay with the company (3%).

Feeling underpromoted and unappreciated is frustrating and a serious problem at any age but can take on a deeper significance in later years when the position at which one is stuck may well turn out to be one's last job before retirement. The majority of older managers interviewed said that they wouldn't mind further promotion but that this was unlikely (26%). Reactions to this situation varied considerably – but 'realistic' acceptance was the main theme of intent, if not emotional practice. Those who had come to a standstill looked for what novelty and expansion there was in their current job (6%), were glad to have achieved so much (8.5%), welcomed the opportunity to devote more time to their families (6%) and applied for other jobs but with little hope of success (3%); but several showed a dampened enthusiasm and cynicism which had repercussions both at work and home (8.5%). Having experienced a job move which was seen as demotion was less likely to be treated philosophically. Only one manager accepted this 'gracefully', welcoming the reduced time pressure. The remainder found it impossible to reduce their job involvement from its previously high (and well-rewarded) level to that currently required by the company. Having responsibility but no authority, irritation at the loss of status symbols – carpets, etc. or budgetary control – needing to hide one's disappointment from wife and family, trying to develop compensatory creative hobbies and worries that one might lose 'the little one has' were symptoms of this syndrome. It would appear that this situation is inevitable (perhaps increasingly) for considerable numbers of managers who cannot achieve their (perhaps 'unrealistic') ambitions. It is obviously more painful if career ceiling is reached 10 to 15 years or more before retirement and the manager's lack of insight and/or the company's ambiguous messages contrive to make this 'fact' less than obvious.

Several managers in anticipation of fewer opportunities at higher levels voiced plans to leave the company later on (11%) – to go into a smaller firm where they could be top more easily, to start their own business as a change or to pursue a less competitive career such as technical writing. For the majority however the main method of trying to assure job security and enhance career development chances was to work harder and ensure that they performed well in their current positions.

PRESSURES ASSOCIATED WITH THE WORK:HOME INTERFACE

Throughout the above sections, the implication has been that managers in the sample had extremely demanding jobs to which they were heavily committed. A focal concern during interviewing was therefore to discover how this affected their home lives and what balance they managed to achieve between the two life areas. No attempt was made to assess the 'quality' of the couples' marriages, a factor which will obviously be of paramount importance here. Many appeared to be 'happily married', the majority 'satisfied' (at varying levels of joint involvement and concern). Whilst a few showed tensions at the time of contact it was impossible to do more than speculate as to the extent or effects of these. Those who had achieved a mutually acceptable ordering of priorities and were able to implement this seemed to have fewer problems that those for whom this was a constant topic of 'negotiation'.

A. TAKING WORK HOME

Except in production jobs (described above) and when they have to attend social engagements (in themselves mentioned as a pressure by 16% of the interviewees), managers tend to do extra work at home rather than on site. Wives preferred this arrangement (8.5%) and it enabled managers to keep relatively 'normal hours' except that work rather than leisure activities dominated their evenings and often their weekends.

Many admitted to taking 'a lot' of work home (37%) and others 'quite a bit' (8.5%); a minority said that they tried not to (6%) or that doing so was a sign of not being able to do one's job properly (3%). Work at two extremes of the spectrum is involved – routine paperwork (17%) and keeping up to date with journal articles, etc. (6%), as there was no time to do this during the day, and things which required special attention such as report writing (6%) and preparing material for meetings (14%) – 'it's impossible to concentrate at work'. For the most part managers said that they didn't mind taking work home and implied that work was an 'acceptable' spare-time activity. There were however expressions of resentment if weekends were affected (20%), complaints that out-of-work activities, especially sports, were severely restricted (6%), that working 7-day weeks for a long period can have serious build-up effects (3%), reports that work is taken home only because everyone else does so (3%) and it is 'the only way to keep up' (6%). There is an obvious danger that norms for performance will be set too high: it seems that for this group they have indeed escalated, pushed on perhaps by the over-zealous and those with no out-of-work interest, leaving 'the average manager' no alternative but to conform. As showing signs of weakness is 'inadmissable', the individual manager has little opportunity to assess the overall situation or power to act to alter it.

Wives were a little less accepting than their husbands of this intrusion of work into home life and many had found it necessary to develop their own separate lives and social activities to keep them occupied in the evenings. Several were concerned about the effects bringing work home had on their husbands' general well-being (14%) – especially when this involved getting up at 4 o'clock in the morning or not feeling able to switch off when visitors were there. Work appeared in fact to be the sample's main leisure activity and the managers reported having no time for (other) hobbies (20%), car maintenance (3%), cutting the grass (3%) or to get involved with the local community (6%).

B. BUSINESS TRAVEL

Another major job element which has important repercussions on home life is business travel. The sample's jobs varied widely in the amount required – from occasional only to frequent international trips.

Whilst travel can be enjoyable (6%), good for the manager (3%) and be welcomed for a short time for the freedom it offers (14%), it was more of note for its negative effects. For the manager these were:

   losing work time (11%)

   having to travel in one's own time (8.5%)

   that travel is 'boring' (8.5%) as one does not see the places involved anyway (3%)

   wearying time distortions (6%)

   possibly missing important stages in his children's development (8.5%) (their birth or first day at school for example), or being away when they are ill and he is needed (3%) which later affects relationships (6%) and causes regret

For the wife the negative effects were:

   having to take on all the responsibility for the family especially when there were young children (32%)

   being a more stable influence (7%)

   exerting more discipline (7%)

if separation is for several months (even with weekend contact), finding this particularly traumatic (25%)

Most wives come to accept their husband's absences; some like to have an evening to themselves and even take pride in their ability to cope alone. They may still however envy him the travel (and feeling of doing something important) involved in his job and express the wish to go too (11%). Husbands who had particularly acute work:home conflict problems also thought that this might help (8.5%).

The common themes of the above two sections have been time-management and work:home conflict problems. It was obvious that for the majority of the sample work ruled their day-to-day lives (40%) and that 'top jobs' required total commitment (14%). Family life has to be organised around the manager's commitments (26%) although it is usually difficult to *plan* anything except at weekends and his wife's social life is drastically curbed as a result (20%).

Most wives (especially those in the older age groups whose approach to marriage is more traditional) accepted this ordering of priorities and saw their main purposes as being to support their husbands, freeing them to work hard and also organising some sort of out-of-work social life for them. On a subjective assessment only 29%(*) of all the wives classified were not actively 'supportive' in this way at the time of contact:

TABLE 5.1 Subjective classification of wives' roles in relation to their husband's work

Housewife		Working wife	
'Support team'	= 55%	but Supportive	= 16%
*Frustrated career woman	= 10%	*Working out new home: work balance	= 6%
		*Independent	= 13%

Most were however insistent that they needed some independent activities as a source of satisfaction and to alleviate boredom as long as this did not interfere with their primary role as wife. In only a minority of cases had this need for self-fulfilment diverted the wife's attention from her husband and family. This theme of managerial marriage patterns is taken up again and discussed in more detail later.

In return most of the managers' excess time and energy are devoted to their wives and families – they see themselves as being very home-oriented although some do find time for sports – particularly golf. Only 13% said that they felt they seriously neglected their wives and children and in one case this was for sports rather than work activities. One manager expressed the view, which most others seemed to hold, that it was all right for work to take up one's social life but 'dangerous' when it started to divert attention from the family.

Their homes were extremely important to managers as a place in which they could switch off and the majority separated home from work (60%) (taking papers, reports, etc. home was not considered to be a violation of this separation) as a way of preserving the boundaries of their sanctuary. Separation was in fact achieved in three ways:

   i. by adopting the policy of living well away from the site (11%)
  ii. by endeavouring not to mix socially with other company employees (34%)
iii. chiefly, by not discussing work with one's wife (47%)

This 'silence' is more on job content than interpersonal issues (many managers thought that their wives could be of help with the latter) and the following explanatory reasons were given:

work is confidential (14%)
'I don't like to tell her my worries' (14%)
'She's not interested' (11%) (especially in getting involved socially)
'She wouldn't understand' (11%)
'She has her own problems' (3%), and
'She's more help that way' (3%)

From comparing husbands' and wives' reports it also appeared that managers were not always open with their wives about career hopes and opportunities particularly if these were likely to involve a move she might be reluctant to make. They preferred to cross difficult bridges when they came to them!

Some wives said that they would like to have known more about what was going on and to have become more involved in company life (18%) but appreciated their husbands' need to segregate these two life areas.

A minority of couples were happy to integrate work and home life; wives became involved in and enjoyed social activities (mostly at senior managerial levels where this was to a certain extent required) and work was an accepted topic of conversation (17%).

Even if they tried to separate work and home most managers found that their experiences during the day played a large part in determining their mood in the evenings ('inability to switch off' is discussed in the section concerning individual characteristics below).

'Stress at work' appears to have different outcomes depending on its cause and the personality of the manager concerned – two basic syndromes were apparent: (1) being bad-tempered, irritable, wanting to be alone (34%) (one manager suggested that this was the result of bottling-up tension and aggression at work) or (2) being depressed, too tired to do anything and 'taking the easy way out' in leisure activities (23%). Typically wives took on a protective role in such circumstances – trying not 'to take it personally', keeping the children away and coping with what has to be done – although several implied that after a while they would put pressure on their husbands to 'shake out of it'.

C. THE EFFECTS OF HOME LIFE ON THE MANAGER

As one would expect influence can also be in the reverse direction as problems at home affect the manager and eventually feed back to his work performance. The most important factor at home in this regard is his wife's happiness. As the interviews concentrated on work experiences and relocations it was such issues which were mentioned as influences in this context – the following 'list' is, therefore, by no means exhaustive. Several young wives found the role of 'housewife and trapped mother' frustrating and wanted to go out to work as soon as possible (14%). Whilst their husbands were not entirely to blame for their situation it was apparent that the issue was a cause of some tension especially if a recent move or inappropriate house choice (e.g. in a lonely area) was accentuating the problem. Several older wives also had problems in relation to work. Some were bored at home and their husbands would have liked them to take jobs and be less emotionally and financially dependent (21%) (older managers' career frustrations appeared to be aggravated if their wives too were wholly dependent for satisfaction on their success) – several however doubted their competence to do so (11%). Managers whose wives (of all ages) did, or wanted to, work were extremely conscious of the risk that their and their family's home comforts would suffer and several wives were criticised for a tendency to become too involved in their jobs (18%). Most husbands however found that the benefits outweighed the organisational problems involved as their wives gained self-confidence: 'she became the woman I married'.

Concern about children – excessive 'sensitivity', schooling problems, rebellious teenagers – were also expressed by managers but appeared to be less immediate worries perhaps because such responsibilities were largely shouldered by their wives. Children were said to make more demands (on time) as they got older (14%) (this could be a good outlet from work) and family responsibilities could reduce career freedom (7%) and make managing on one income difficult (7%).

Most of the sample lived away from their parents and this separation could impose a further home-related strain at times (11%). Several had had to take in and care for an ailing parent (11%) and whilst they accepted this it had restricted their freedom particularly when moving.

INDIVIDUAL CHARACTERISTICS AS CAUSES OF STRESS

The final category of pressures are internal rather than external forces. Whilst no assessment of personality was made during the qualitative data-collection phase it was apparent that individual differences were of extreme importance. Many managers for example reported their inability 'to switch off' in the evenings (40%) (only 28% said that this was easy) finding that even whilst they watched television they could not stop thinking about work. Some accepted and enjoyed this as a natural result of their satisfying involvement in work ('the more you put in, the more you get out') but many would have preferred to have more self-control. Several interviewees expressed concern that they were letting work play too dominant a role in their lives (11%) and those who said that the company was not 'a way of life' (8.5%) did so with some pride.

In the section on workload, 'personality reasons' for becoming overwhelmed by overload were mentioned – these were the conscientious, self-critical and perfectionist approach which a substantial number of managers adopted to life in general and work in particular. This personality type (26%) typically became highly involved in work (perhaps taking on more than they could later cope with), believed that every job should be done well, put pressure on themselves to achieve high standards and felt guilty at not working when more was waiting to be done. Managers in this 'group' were particularly likely to sacrifice home for work life but in general their wives valued their drive and dedication (whilst regretting some of its effects) and offered little resistance. Whilst it is unlikely that this life style will be good for the manager in the long-term, his short-term work performance and job satisfaction are greatly enhanced; for its part the company appears willing to accept all that he is prepared to give and does not know the extent of the effort required.

Interview data also supported the suggestion that certain personality characteristics may fit particularly well or poorly with a given set of job demands (P:E fit). It was common for example to find scientists and technologists promoted to jobs which involved considerable responsibility for people. Some welcomed this new focus but others had problems in deciding what were the truly important aspects of their work and how they should apportion their time.

AN OVERVIEW OF MANAGERIAL PRESSURE

So far in this chapter work pressures have been described for the most part stripped of their context. Whilst this is inevitable with the analytic approach adopted (which is the only practical way of dealing with such an overwhelming mass of data) some attempt must be made to capture the gestalt of these experiences. Below 'job satisfactions' are reported, briefly, as a 'balance'. Managers attitudes to these pressures can also help to put them in perspective. Taking a broad view they can be placed on two underlying continua. The first reflects 'acceptability' – some pressures were seen as being an inevitable part of the job, 'What I'm paid for', and thus more acceptable; others as unnecessary obstructions to doing one's job well. The second reflects their contribution to satisfaction – some were 'challenges', others could not be successfully overcome.

In the following figure pressure areas are assigned to quadrants rather than scale positions.

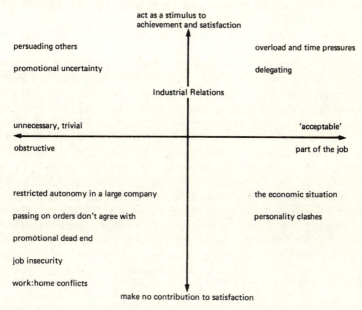

FIGURE 5.1 Classification of job areas by managers' attitudes

MANAGERIAL JOB SATISFACTION

As promised, the overall emphasis of this chapter has been towards work pressure; interviewees were also asked what they enjoyed about their jobs and these replies are reported briefly here.

The most frequently quoted satisfactions from work were 'pay' (43%) and the high standard of living this secured (28.5%). Many reported having been relatively 'poor' in their early years with the company and were more than content with the financial rewards committed service had brought them. (There was an awareness however that in the short term at least their privileged status was being eroded by successive economic crises and government 'attacks' on the middle classes.)

A second cluster of satisfactions are related to job content; having a 'challenging' (14%), 'interesting' (6%) 'varied' (6%) or 'creative' (3%) job were all mentioned. In a similar vein managers reported enjoying solving problems (mostly technical) (17%), achieving production or other objective targets (17%) or making a decision that turned out to be right (6%). Several remembered their early days with the company as being particularly filled with such experiences. Starting things (20%) – whether it was a new plant or an accounts system – was exciting 'leaving no time for anything else'; it meant autonomy, 'I didn't have to refer any decisions to anyone' and working as a member/leader of a team, 'we had no personnel problems then'.

Managers were also pleased by promotion (17%) – it shows that superiors think they are capable, means more pay and 'another step up the ladder'; it is particularly significant if it is 'faster than the norm' or leads to 'the job I had my eye on'. With higher managerial level having power brings added rewards (37%) – making an impact ('there are things *I* can do that matter'), making important decisions, influencing strategy or other people and implementing changes. Independence and autonomy, mostly as a result of an immediate superior's non-interference, were also highly prized (26%) – managers valued their freedom to do a 'whole' job and to operate within their 'own area of authority'. Short-stay jobs abroad were particularly praised as involving considerable authority and responsibility for their official level (14%).

Interviewees saw large-company membership as having considerable advantages (28.5%) – providing security, facilitating contact with a wide range of other function groups and offering a wide range of travel, experience and career opportunities. There was evidence of the potential for personal growth in such an environment, growth which may not only benefit the employee but also, through his increased confidence and sensitivity, his wife and family. Managers, even those in service departments, also derived satisfaction from involvement in an end-product (17%). Interviewees of both sexes mentioned the family atmosphere that prevails in the company and felt that the latter attracts interesting, friendly people (17%). In view of this, satisfaction from one's work team (11%) and managing people (17%) are obvious additional positive elements.

Relating these satisfactions back to the job areas already mentioned as pressures we find:

a. that some pressures also cause satisfaction – e.g. job challenges, people–management problems
b. some job areas are almost solely stressful – time demands, overload and the consequent home:work conflicts
c. others almost solely satisfying – relationships
d. career development is a crucial factor – much of the manager's ac-

tivity is geared to enhancing his progress and it is particularly difficult to adapt to thwarted ambitions

e. that personality and environmental factors interplay to determine the individual's involvement in his job and his perception of it.

COPING

Whilst the question was seldom asked directly some evidence as to how managers cope with work pressures was revealed. It will already be evident that by far the most common technique was to work longer hours. Other ways of coping with overload were delegation (6%), negotiating and compromising with those setting work to produce only that which is really needed (8.5%), redistributing workload within the department (6%), planning ahead to annual demand peaks (3%), and balancing the department's internally and externally generated load (3%).

Various strategies were adopted in answer to other pressures:

experts are on hand in the company to help answer work-content queries (6%)

'talking things over' can help with relationships problems (3%)

inadequate information can be covered up temporarily by stalling (3%)

reverting to an authoritarian management style can help one over 'a particularly bad patch' (3%).

On a more general level 'flex time' was praised for solving work:home time conflicts (8.5%) and physical work for acting as an outlet for built-up frustrations (8.5%) – 'I resolve more personnel problems when digging the garden than . . . .'

Another factor which appeared to act as a 'safety valve' was the preservation of a stability area which afforded security and an assured identity uncontaminated by work. For many managers this was home life (discussed in detail above) and their wives sanctioned and fostered this 'sectioning off' – the church and sports activities also played a part for some individuals.

SUMMARY

Issues are covered in their order of appearance in the text. Whilst it is not possible to rank job pressures and satisfactions as to their importance some indication of this is given by the use of an asterisk to denote majority (versus minority) concerns.

JOB PRESSURES

    i. Different groups have distinct 'job stress profiles' – it was possible to describe in detail those for service and production departments

•ii. Only four of the sample did not complain of work overload. Individual differences appear to influence the ability to 'control' this pressure

•iii. Overload led to time pressures

    iv. People–management was a pressure in two contexts –
        Industrial relations – these acted for some as a stimulating and for others as a frustrating job element – and Coping with work delegation.

•v. For some top managers promotion brings the need to develop a new and surprising job skill – the ability to persuade others.

Further pressures were:

    vi. the general economic situation

    vii. restricted autonomy in a big company

    viii. passing on orders and implementing policies one doesn't agree with.

•ix. Concerns about career development were of three kinds –
        general uncertainty about career prospects and a need to pay continual attention to them
        having reached a promotional dead end and
        fears of job loss or early retirement.

    x. 'Personality clashes' were also causes of pressure.

•xi. Achieving an acceptable (to self and wife) balance between work and home life was a problem for many, particularly with regard to the common need to disrupt the latter by taking work home and business travel, the majority of managers' preference for segregating the two areas and their wives' and families' needs for life satisfaction.

    xii. Most wives accept and many actively support the domination of their joint lives by their husband's work.

    xiii. Individual differences play an obvious but at this stage unassessed part in mediating job pressure.

JOB SATISFACTIONS

•i. pay and a high standard of living

•ii. challenging job aspects

    iii. promotion *per se*

    iv. 'having an impact'

v. independence and autonomy
vi. security and scope of working for a large company.

COPING

*i. The most common method of coping with overload was to work longer hours.

6 Issues Raised by an Examination of Managers Under Pressure

The aim of this chapter is to draw together the research results and consider their practical and conceptual implications. First a model of the causation of work stress will be described based on the study reported in this book. This will help us to understand more clearly the predictive power of person and environmental factors for different managerial functions and levels. Turning to more conceptual issues, the use of the terms 'stress' and 'satisfaction' are explored and a tentative paradigm incorporating both states presented. The roles adopted by managers' wives were not an original research concern but proved of considerable importance in the context of stress (for both partners). The next chapter describes contemporary changes in these roles and the implications for managers both in their marriages and in their work for the company. Next the methodology and techniques used are discussed in terms of their weaknesses and strengths and some suggestions made for future research along similar and complementary lines. Finally, in chapter 8, possible stress prevention programmes for managers are discussed.

A MODEL OF WORK STRESS

With the limited comparative data available we have not found that the sample of managers studied are more stressed than population norms. At an absolute level they do however report sufficient work pressures to suggest that their lives need not be as stressful as they are. What model of the causes of stress, on the basis of this work, can we build up? We must firstly consider the conceptual issue of whether the Person:Environment fit model, which guided the research design, is (in the light of results) still appropriate:

1. Initial multiple regression analyses suggested that personality alone was a sufficient predictor of stress symptoms but it would appear that this conclusion was an artefact of treating as an entity a group within which there are significantly different sub-

populations. More detailed analyses showed that 'vulnerability' is important but that it seldom acts irrespective of external pressures.

2. In the majority of analyses therefore both systems in interaction determined stress scores (though one or the other may dominate in any given set of circumstances). This supports the impression gained during interviewing.

3. In several analyses examination of the wider work context and not merely the manager's immediate work situation proved necessary to achieve a full understanding of the development of stress symptoms. It would appear therefore that the P:E fit model provides an adequate structure in terms of which job stress can be described and investigated but that 'macro' as well as 'micro' environmental factors must be considered. A distinction between these two levels of environmental influence is therefore made in the following sections, the former including particularly the 'given' conditions of company structure and climate.

Before going on to describe the P:E combinations associated with stress symptoms for the sample it is appropriate to summarise the research design in the terminology used. Figure 6.1 positions the independent variables, used here as potential causes of stress, in the P:E fit framework. The job and organisational factors derived from factor analysis of the Job Characteristics Questionnaire have been 'neutralised' (i.e. a single label has been used for each bipolar scale) to depict 'dimensions' on which jobs are assessed rather than indicate pressure or satisfaction from these dimensions. Several career demographic items are very similar to derived factor themes and an attempt has been made to align related items. See Fig. 6.1, p. 98.

The two dependent stress measures will continue to be treated separately. Whilst there is evidence of considerable overlap between them, several findings show that they are not consistently closely linked. For example correlations between anxiety and physical ill-health are non-significant for two of the five job function groups suggesting that interdependence between psychological and physical health may be another important individual difference to be borne in mind. Also there is tentative evidence that the two syndromes are caused by different environmental pressures. In view of these findings we shall continue to treat anxiety and physical ill-health as distinguishable stress reactions in the analyses which follow.

Using the P:E fit framework and the statistical findings of Chapter 4 we arrive at the following stress prediction models, firstly for the sample as a whole and then for job function and managerial level sub-groups. The profiles of 'individuals at risk' have already been described in detail above. Here they are simplified to show the critical person and job en-

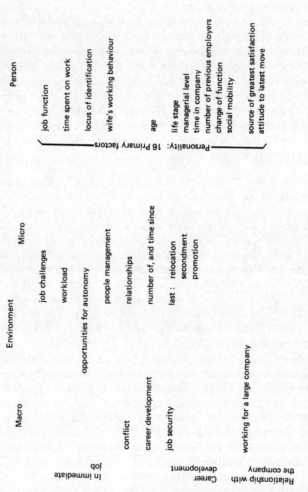

FIGURE 6.1 Orientation of the study's independent variables in the 'macro:micro environment:person' fit framework

vironment variables, values of which can be used to predict whether a particular individual in a particular situation will or will not show stress symptoms (Table 6.1). Predictive power will be limited by the particular equation's adequacy in explaining stress scores' variance. For a general sample member (i.e. one for whom neither job function nor managerial level are known) approximately 70% of the score variance was outside the scope of the variables studied and any prediction would be open to considerable error. Within meaningful population sub-groups more reliable conclusions can be reached. Examining the variables included in the various models we find that in 17 out of the 18 'cases' personality traits play a part. The full range of job and organisational factors appear in interaction with them but certain dimensions – workload, job challenges, opportunities for autonomy and working for a large company – are repeated frequently indicating that these are of more general relevance.

The pressures identified here operate through a mix of influences:

through the 'given' conditions of company structure and practices, job descriptions, etc.

through 'higher management' who set work, restrain individual independence and control rewards

through formal and informal norms against which work performance, job involvement and social behaviour are judged and

through the manager himself as he seeks pressure as stimulation and/or his personality characteristics make him 'stress prone' by being anxious, ambitious or poorly suited to his job demands.

(They operate also at two stages in the stress sequence. Not only are person and environment factors initiating *causes* of stress, they also influence the individual's ability to cope later on. This point will be considered in more depth below.) We can expect these same four 'levels of action' (again as a 'mix') to be appropriate when we consider below potential 'cures' for stress within the organisation.

'STRESS' AND 'SATISFACTION'

Use of the term and concept 'stress' was considered in depth during the development of our research proposals and results afforded us the opportunity of examining the relationship between the two dimensions measured, psychological and physical stress manifestations. We find that whilst they are related, correspondence between them is by no means perfect. For the sample as a whole the correlation between the two scores was 0.47 but the significance of this relationship was maintained

TABLE 6.1 Critical person and environment variables predicting psychological and physical health

	Environment Macro	Environment Micro	Person	Predictive of
Total sample	Workload Opportunities for autonomy		Personality: Forthright *vs* shrewd less intelligent *vs* more intelligent	→ Psychological Health
			Personality: affected by feelings *vs* emotionally stable toughminded *vs* tenderminded relaxed *vs* tense humble *vs* assertive	→ Physical Health
Research Manager		People-management No of relocations	Personality: humble *vs* assertive toughminded *vs* tenderminded group dependent *vs* self-sufficient Age Smoking behviour Time spent on work	→ Psychological Health
	Working for a large company	People-management No. of secondments	Personality: less intelligent *vs* more intelligent group dependent *vs* self-sufficient undisciplined self-conflict *vs* controlled Source of satisfaction	→ Physical Health

Production Manager

Job security
Working for a large company
Opportunities for autonomy

No. of secondments
Workload
Job challenges

Personality:
reserved *vs* outgoing
group dependent *vs* self-sufficient

→ Psychological Health

Personality:
affected by feelings *vs* emotionally stable
humble *vs* assertive
less intelligent *vs* more intelligent
Managerial level
Age
Smoking behaviour
Wife's 'occupation'

Personality:
forthright *vs* shrewd

→ Physical Health

Service Manager

Opportunities for autonomy

Working for a large company
Time since relocation
Time since promotion

Opportunities for autonomy

Personality:
relaxed *vs* tense
humble *vs* assertive
affected by feelings *vs* emotionally stable

→ Psychological Health

→ Physical Health

TABLE 6.1—*Continued*

	Environment		Person	Predictive of
	Macro	*Micro*		
Marketing Manager		Workload Time since relocation Job challenges	Personality: forthright *vs* shrewd reserved *vs* outgoing	→ Psychological Health
		Job challenges	Personality: affected by feelings *vs* emotionally stable tough-minded *vs* tenderminded relaxed *vs* tense Source of satisfaction	→ Physical Health
Engineering Manager	Opportunities for autonomy	Job challenges	Personality: less intelligent *vs* more intelligent Age Managerial level Source of satisfaction	→ Psychological Health
	Job security	Job challenges	Personality: placid *vs* apprehensive practical *vs* imaginative undisciplined self conflict *vs* controlled tough-minded *vs* tender-minded	→ Physical Health
Lower Management	Conflict	Workload	Personality: forthright *vs* shrewd conservative *vs* experimenting less intelligent *vs* more intelligent	→ Psychological Health

	Factors	Personality	Health outcome
Intermediate Management	Conflict Workload Job challenges	Personality: affected by feelings *vs* emotionally stable tough-minded *vs* tender-minded relaxed *vs* tense humble *vs* assertive practical *vs* experimenting	→ Physical Health
	Opportunities for autonomy Working for a large company Career development	Personality: forthright *vs* shrewd less intelligent *vs* more intelligent	→ Psychological Health
Top Management	Career development Time since relocation Relationships	Personality: placid *vs* apprehensive tough-minded *vs* tender-minded	→ Physical Health
	Working for a large company	Smoking behaviour	→ Psychological Health
	Time since promotion No. of relocations Working for a large company Conflict	Personality: affected by feelings *vs* emotionally stable trusting *vs* suspicious Age	→ Physical Health

for only three of the five function sub-groups. This, and the supporting finding that if we isolate the 18% or so scoring highest on each stress criterion scale only 34% of the 47 individuals thus identified scored at the extreme end of *both* scales, shows that for substantial numbers of the sample mental and physical ill-health are not closely associated and suggests that their relationship is in fact an important individual difference. The 'ability' to separate these two dimensions of functioning may in fact have certain 'benefits'. Both functions who did so – research and production – appeared to be relatively immune to intrinsically stressful job demands and scored significantly below other groups on the anxiety scale.

A related area of interest is at what phase of the stress sequence the two types of symptom occur; does one for example play a part in causing the other. As no longitudinal data was collected discussion of this issue can only be speculative. Considering the possible relationships of the two classes of symptom included for study, four sequential 'models' can be hypothesised – these are shown in Figure 6.2. The findings support (however tentatively) three of these and do nothing to refute the fourth.

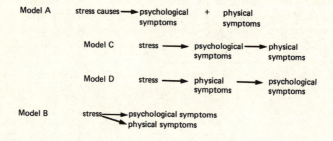

FIGURE 6.2 The sequence of stress symptoms – four possible models

As mental and physical health appear to be closely associated for some members of the sample but not for others both general models A and B – that psychological and physical symptoms are additive and that they are alternatives, respectively – are in fact 'confirmed' by the data. The latter is also supported by the earlier conclusion that different sorts of stress ('active' versus 'passive' in the profile of the production manager) may result in different types of symptom. Whilst it would appear likely that for those who 'subscribe' to model A, anxiety plays some part in the development of physical illness (stress by definition is psychologically mediated) the statistical evidence for this – in several multiple regression equations anxious personality factors were associated with poor physical

health scores – is far from sample-wide. Several interviewees did
however confirm such a sequence in reports of specific illnesses which
had followed particularly stressful periods at work. Finally whilst the
findings of this study do not directly confirm the path of action depicted
by model D (that physical symptoms cause anxiety) it does have commonsense 'appeal' and can not therefore be rejected outright. It must
therefore be concluded that not only the 'causative' person:environ-
ment combination but also the display of different types of stress symptoms is highly situation- and person-specific and that models of the
stress sequence must be sufficiently flexible to mirror this variability.

Use of the term 'satisfaction', initially taken for granted, can also be
reviewed in the light of results. On the Job Characteristics Questionnaire managers found no difficulty in rating degrees of 'satisfaction'
('Something you enjoy which contributes to your sense of achievement')
used as an external force as was 'pressure'; 'satisfaction' is also commonly used to refer to the state to which 'stress' is the complement.
Looked at from the point of view of the level of activation involved the
state of satisfaction is generally implied to be at the lower end of the
scale. (Roget's Thesaurus 1966, associates it with 'contentment; com-
placency; serenity'.) We do not feel however that the majority of
managers were using it in this way – they were referring rather to
stimulating satisfaction. The state of satisfaction, like that of stress,
denotes a range of emotional experiences, and two-dimensional rather
than one-dimensional modelling becomes necessary to relate these concepts, superseding the high stimulation stress–low stimulation satisfaction continuum implicit in much of the literature. Figure 6.3 depicts the
proposed relationship taking activation level and affect as the two axes.

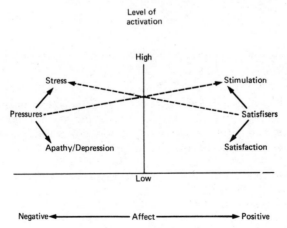

FIGURE 6.3 The hypothesised relationship between stress and satisfaction; as
external forces and states of the organism

An attempt has been made to distinguish the four potential states and their external causes linguistically. Referring back to the multiple regression analyses (the 'ability' of both pressures and satisfactions to cause harm) and bearing in mind the psychological and physical correlates of high activation levels, we find that results support the possibility that the latter is a more important cause of damage than the affect involved (satisfaction from having a challenging job is a notable contributor to high stress scores for example). If this is so it means that our measures of, and definition of, 'stress' are 'at odds' in that the former fails to distinguish between positive and negative causative experiences whereas the latter does so. In order to complete the diagram it is therefore necessary to indicate that 'satisfisers' contribute to negative outcomes, and pressures (as has already been accepted) complementarily contribute to positive outcomes – these 'extra' lines of action are here shown by dotted lines.

The Roles Adopted by Managers' Wives

Interviews with managers' wives revealed a wide range of differing 'home circumstances'. In particular if the wives of today's junior managers are also considered (these are the 'non-senior staff' group interviewed primarily with reference to relocation experiences and therefore excluded from the data base of the above qualitative results section) it becomes apparent that changes in society's values are having a marked impact on the roles of 'husband' and 'wife'. The main development important to the topic of this book as it vitally effects 'how well' he is able to do his job is the trend for the manager's wife to pay more attention to fulfilling her own needs for work satisfaction outside the home and less to supporting her husband in performance of his job. Looking at the total interview sample a pattern emerged in the roles wives occupied, and reported occupying at previous life stages, and this is represented diagrammatically in Figure 7.1. Roles are depicted by boxes and organised along two axes: a time dimension from the past to the future and the family life cycle from 'early marriage' through 'childbearing and rearing' to the 'empty nest' (i.e. couples with children at home but relatively independent and those whose children have moved away). The thin lines and arrows in the diagram indicate possible paths of progression from one role to another. This typology of managers' wives' roles will now be described and some of its implications for wives, husbands and organisations which employ the latter discussed:

Boxes A, B, C, D and H are sufficient to describe the present and past roles of the vast majority of the wives of today's senior managers, the older interviewees. The progression from A to B to C is 'traditional' for this middle-class group. The wife typically gives up her job when she marries to become a full-time housewife, her 'true' vocation. Marriage is not usually as exciting and fulfilling as she had expected and this may be a particularly lonely time for her (especially if promotions move the couple away from her supportive family and friends and into hostile, 'non-mobile' areas of the country). Whilst the housewife may envy her husband his job and freedom she fundamentally accepts her role as a

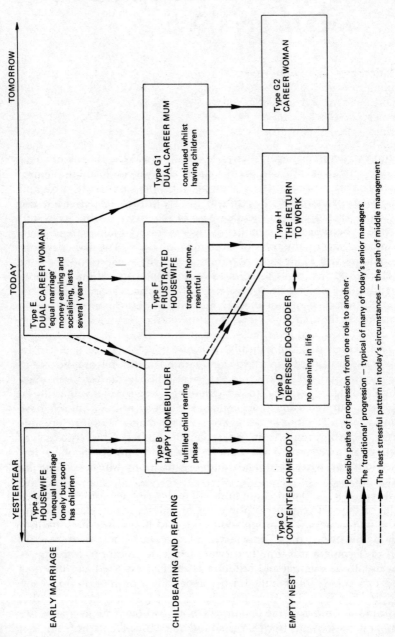

FIGURE 7.1 Roles 'open' to the manager's wife

YESTERYEAR — TODAY — TOMORROW

EARLY MARRIAGE

Type A
HOUSEWIFE
'unequal marriage'
lonely but soon
has children

Type E
DUAL CAREER WOMAN
'equal marriage'
money earning and
socialising, lasts
several years

Type G1
DUAL CAREER MUM
continued whilst
having children

Type G2
CAREER WOMAN

CHILDBEARING AND REARING

Type B
HAPPY HOMEBUILDER
fulfilled child rearing
phase

Type F
FRUSTRATED
HOUSEWIFE
trapped at home,
resentful

EMPTY NEST

Type C
CONTENTED HOMEBODY

Type D
DEPRESSED DO-GOODER
no meaning in life

Type H
THE RETURN
TO WORK

Possible paths of progression from one role to another.

The 'traditional' progression — typical of many of today's senior managers.

The least stressful pattern in today's circumstances — the path of middle management supportive wife and housekeeper and looks forward to starting a family. Being a happy homebuilder is therefore a demanding but fulfilling time for her. The young wife's preoccupation now parallels her husband's involvement in his work and the couple are likely to cope with their workloads and stresses separately. The role segregation in which this results probably means that psychologically they seldom 'meet'; their relationships are complementary rather than shared. If the wife is willing to continue to maintain a supportive role vis-à-vis her husband as the children become independent and move away from home she can be described as a 'contented homebody'. She may take on outside activities – the Women's Institute, voluntary social work, flower arranging and the like – to help fill her day but her main concern will be that these should not interfere with the (limited) time she spends with her husband. In this type of marriage the couple continue in their complementary roles; his career success satisfies them both (she may well take on a social role in relation to his job) and the organisation benefits by getting one and a half employees for the price of one.

Types D and H deviate somewhat from this traditional pattern. There is little to distinguish the depressed do-gooder from the contented homebody in the way she spends her day – the fundamental difference is however that the former does not find the things she does fulfilling. Whilst the latter has built up a meaningful identity the former has somehow failed to do so. At this stage many wives take on a job, usually part-time, to fill the gap in their lives (the 'return to work') and although they may have initial problems in balancing home and work demands find that both they and their husbands benefit from their decision to do so. For those who cannot take such a step this can be an exceptionally unhappy and depressing time. Their husbands may not be sympathetic to these rather vague identity problems or may be going through similar problems of their own and the couples' segregated past has given them little practice in dealing with such interpersonal problems.

The common factor in these five boxes is the agreement by manager, wife and his employing company that his job dominates the couples' lives. It is this basic tenet that younger generations are questioning and their differences of opinion is reflected in the new, alternative roles they have opened up. Today's junior manager is likely to marry a dual career wife. More widely available higher education, the need for two incomes to accumulate capital and their failure to find being 'just a housewife' a meaningful identity prompt most women to continue working after marriage. The wife's attitude at this stage is a key to the couple's future. For many women job soon takes second place to husband and home and they opt happily for, and derive pleasure from, the happy homebuilder role when it arrives, usually planning to return to work when their children reach senior school age. At the other extreme is the dual career orientation. The wife is heavily involved in her job and continues to work returning soon after having children if the couple choose to do so. The working woman is in a position of obvious role conflict and the relationship she achieves with her husband will depend largely on his expectations of her as a wife (and mother of his children). A consistent complaint of those managers whose wives worked (at any life stage) was that they became 'too involved' in the jobs they did. Very few men were prepared to share home-maintaining activities and make the sacrifices in home comforts that having a career-oriented wife necessitated. 'Women's Liberation' has thrown men's as much as women's roles into confusion. A critical decision is whether or not to have children. It is those women who decide to do so and then find themselves trapped by their decision who are the casualties of 'the new mores' and are labelled frustrated housewives here. These women not only do not enjoy the day-to-day activities of running a home and raising a family but feel that they are actually suffering from the experience. At the same time a conscientious approach to motherhood prevents them from escaping. A wife in this situation may well jealously vent some of her 'wrath' on her husband by actively withholding her support; rather than helping him cope with work stress she adds to his problems. The strain this situation puts on the couple's relationship may well only be removed by time when the wife eventually comes to feel that she will not be neglecting her children by returning to work.

The dotted line in Figure 7.1 shows the least stressful pattern in today's circumstances; but whatever the role his wife adopts we see that today's manager is likely to have less time and energy to devote to work and to receive less support from home in the performance of his job. Industry for its part appears to be unaware of these changes in its employees' commitments and attitudes and still demands the high involvement it has come to expect. As noted earlier, the majority of those interviewed still subscribed to the old values that the husband's job should 'come first' but many couples (particularly those of lower level staff omitted from the qualitative analysis) were facing the problem of how to cope with a working wife. In the short-term at least the company is likely to find that it 'loses' by these developments as its managers become less able, and probably less willing, to devote themselves wholeheartedly to its goals. In the long-term it may well find that it benefits from the balanced lives they have established (reaching one's career ceiling is particularly likely to be less threatening). It is ironic that the impetus for this development should come not from the over-utilised manager but from his under-utilised wife and is further evidence that underload is as powerfully (perhaps more?) stressful than overload.

8 Managerial Stress Prevention

This material was adapted from work published by the authors in *Management Decision*, vol. 13, no. 5. For a fuller discussion of 'coping with stress; see Cooper and Marshall, *Understanding Executive Stress*, Chapter 7 (1977).

Up to now we have described what we consider to be some of the more important origins of stress and some of their consequences for individuals and organisations. We have even complicated the issue by showing how closely stress is related to satisfaction. A dominant consideration in the reader's mind must now be 'how can we make the effects of stress at work minimally damaging?' both to the individual and the organisation.

If we examine the factors which are intrinsic to the job and the individual there are several possible stress-preventive steps one might consider. Some of the stress research suggests for example that certain types of individuals are more susceptible to stress than others. If an organisation deems the costs of stress too high it has available the possibility of introducing new criteria for selection and placement. It might consider the possibility of trying to select people who are better able to cope with role ambiguity and conflict, with increased responsibility for people, with work overload etc., when these are known to be relevant to a particular job situation. An organisation's ability to optimise the fit between individual and job by their selection procedures will of course depend on extensive validation work on potential selection tests. This is something that will require a great deal of further work but is currently under review by a number of the larger industrial organisations.

Another way of coping with some of the stress associated with the relationship between the individual and the job is by training. Training programmes and techniques are available or could be designed which might help the individual perform his or her job more effectively and with less stress, or to cope with work overload, or to improve his or her relations with others; that is training people to increase their tolerance and coping abilities. Techniques such as TM, role-playing, time management training, personal growth groups, team building activities (as both a source of feedback on the person–job fit and a source of support) and many others are currently available for use in stress prevention and reduction programmes.

'Role in the organisation' is a very important source of stress. Role conflict and ambiguity can be dealt with by procedures designed to clarify the duties (role expectations of others) and performance (role behaviour) of each individual in an organisation. This could be accomplished by encouraging mutual consultation between individual and supervisor for purposes of redefining the job. A systematic procedure of job clarification should help to achieve a somewhat less ambiguous network of interrelated work roles.

It has been suggested (Kahn *et al.*, 1964) that individuals who experience role conflict should be able to confront those making excessive demands on them and 'renegotiate' their relationships. The organisation could help by building in feedback channels of communication which make this possible.

Another important factor associated with the individual's role in the organisation is that of *participation*. Based on our research and number of other research projects (for example French, Kay and Meyer, 1966), we know that stress can result from low participation or lack of autonomy, which leads to job dissatisfaction. The suggestion here is that greater participation in the decision-making process may enhance an individual's own self-esteem and feelings of control and thereby reduce job dissatisfaction and threat. French and Caplan (1973) outline five necessary conditions of any participation programme based on their research findings: first, to reduce stress by increasing participation one must provide a *supportive* supervisor and cohesive work group; second, that participation should *not* be *illusory*, that is that it should not be used as a manipulative tool; third, that the decisions on which participation is based should *not* be *trivial* to the people concerned; fourth, that the decisions should be *relevant*; finally, the decisions should be seen to be a *legitimate* part of their work. These qualifiers are a very useful guide in designing decision-sharing mechanisms particularly in view of recent moves by the government for greater involvement and wider representation in industry.

If we examine the career development factors we can see that some of these (e.g. overpromotion and underpromotion) depend on an accurate assessment by the organisation of the individual's potential and performance at work. Social skill training techniques like sensitivity training (Cooper and Mangham, 1971), team role laboratories (Reddin, 1970) etc. may help to provide those concerned with promotion and management development with the necessary sensitivity to the individual's achievements, potential and other relevant factors in making decisions about promotion. Another important issue that falls within the career development category is job insecurity and fear of redundancy. Many organisations handle this issue very badly indeed. This not only creates a climate of distrust and encourages job dissatisfaction but also is personally damaging to the individual concerned. It seems to us that this is an unnecessary destructive cyclical process, which might be improved by greater openness and honesty on the part of the organisation about issues of job tenure and redundancy. The consequences of mistrust can, as Mellinger (1956) found in a large public research organisation, lead to poor communications and ultimately to bad decision-making.

(O = Organisation, E = Employee):

O mistrusts —> E	E consequently tends to conceal attitudes and information from O by communicating in ways that are: evasive, aggressive, misleading, etc.	—>	O's perception of reality are consequently impaired, e.g. O in cases may overestimate agreement with E or O in cases may underestimate agreement with E

Ineffective communications and lack of trust lead us into another main source of stress – 'poor relations within organisations'. If we are to minimise the potential stress effects of 'being in organisations', with all the behavioural restrictions that implies, and of poor relations between boss and subordinate, and between colleagues, organisations will have to consider change or development programmes that will encourage trust-building activities. Organisational trust-building is characterised by (1) the development of a supportive organisational climate and norms (2) the building of shared norms on the basis of perceived similarities in attitudes and experiences of people working in organisations, and (3) the development of 'we-ness', a shared identity among workers that implies substantial common direction by all (Golembiewski and McConkie, 1975). More and more work is being carried out in the area of organisational change and development to create the conditions of trust and well-being within the workplace (Cooper, 1976) which should help to improve relations between boss and subordinate and between work colleagues, and help to make the constraints associated with living in an organisation less stressful. As Bennis and Slater (1968) suggest in their book on the 'temporary society', industrial life is so fast-moving and changeable that organisations have to adapt by being more flexible and by unfreezing their structures so that individuals are not locked into jobs that might put excessive stress on them. Burns and Stalker (1961) made this point in their book *The Management of Innovation* when they suggested that changing times demand more 'organic' as opposed to 'mechanistic' organisations.

At the moment managers are facing considerable stress at work which is a result of the subtle outgrowth of all the factors discussed in this chapter. Today more organisations are recognising that it is their responsibility to consider these and to help create the conditions for the psychological well-being of their staff. Kornhauser aptly summarised the condition that organisations should be concerned about today:

> 'Mental health is not so much a freedom from specific frustrations as it is an overall balanced relationship to the world which permits a person to maintain realistic, positive belief in himself and his purposeful activities. In so far as his entire job and life situation facilitate and support such feelings of adequacy, inner security and meaningfulness of his existence, it can be presumed that his mental health will tend to be good. What is important in a negative way is not any single characteristic of his situation but everything that deprives the person of purpose and zest, that leaves him with negative feelings about himself, with anxieties, tensions, a sense of lostness, emptiness and futility'.

References

Aldridge, J. F. L., 'Emotional illness and the working environment', *Ergon*, 15 (5) (1970) 613–21.

Altman, I. and Lett, E. E., 'The ecology of interpersonal relationships: a classification system and conceptual model', in J. E. McGrath (ed.), *Social and Psychological Factors in Stress* (New York: Holt, Rinehart and Winston, 1970) pp. 177–201.

Argyris, C., *Integrating the Individual and the Organisation* (New York: Wiley, 1964).

Arnold, M., *Emotion and Personality*, vols. 1 and 2 (New York: Columbia University Press, 1960).

Appley, M. H., 'Motivation, threat perception and the induction of psychological stress', *Proceedings of Sixteenth International Congress of Psychology* (Bonn: Amsterdam: North Holland, 1962) pp. 880–1.

Appley, M. H., 'On the concept of psychological stress'. Paper presented at the *Psychology Colloquium* (State University of New York Buffalo, December, 1964).

Appley, M. H. and Trumbull, R., 'On the concept of psychological stress' in M. H. Appley, and R. Trumbull. *Psychological Stress* (New York: Appleton, 1967).

Appley, M. H. and Trumbull, R., *Psychological Stress* (New York: Appleton, 1967).

Arthur, R. J. and Gunderson, E. K., 'Promotion and mental illness in the Navy', *Journal of Occupational Medicine*, 7 (1965) 452–6.

Bainton, C. R. and Peterson, D. R., 'Deaths from coronary heart disease in persons fifty years of age and younger: A community-wide study', *New Eng. J. Med*, 268 (1963) 569–74.

Bakker, C. B., 'Psychological factors in *agina pectoris*', *Psychosom*, 8 (1967) 43–9.

Bakker, C. B. and Levenson, R. M., 'Determinants of *angina pectoris*', *Psychosom. Med.*, 29 (1967) 621–33.

Barber, R., 'Who would marry a director?' *Director* (March, 1976) pp. 60–2.

Basowitz, H., Persky, H., Korchin, S. J. and Grinker, R. R., *Anxiety and Stress* (New York: McGraw-Hill, 1955).

Beattie, R. T., Darlington, T. G. and Cripps, D. M., *The Management Threshold* (BIM Paper OPN 11, 1974).

Bellotto, S., 'Keeping fit on the executive level', *International Administrative Management*, 32 (February, 1971). 62–3.

Bennis, W. G. and Slater, P. E., *The Temporary Society* (New York: Harper and Row, 1968).

Berkson, D. *et al.,* 'Socioeconomic correlates of atherosclerotic and hypertensive heart disease, in culture, society and health', *Annals of the New York Academy of Sciences*, 84 (1960) 835–50.

Bernard, J., 'The Eudaemonists', in S. Z. Klausner (ed.), *Why Man Takes Chances* (New York: Garden City, 1968) pp. 6–47.

Berry, K. J., 'Status integration and morbidity' (Unpublished Ph.D. Thesis, Corvallis: University of Oregon, 1966).

Birch, S. and Macmillan, B., 'Managers on the Move: a study of British managerial mobility' (BIM Report No. 7, 1970).

Bornstein, M. H. and Bornstein, H. G., 'The pace of city life', *Nature*, 259 (February, 1976) 557–8.

Bortner, R. W. and Rosenman, R. H., 'The measurement of pattern A behaviour', *J. Chron. Dis.*, 20 (1967) 525–33.

Bowlby, J., 'Grief and mourning in infancy and early childhood', *Psychoanalytic Study of the Child*, 15 (1960) 9–52.

Brady, J. V., 'Ulcers in "executive" monkeys', in R. N. Haber (ed.), *Current Research in Motivation* (New York: Holt, Rinehart and Winston, 1966) pp. 242–8.

Braine, J., *Life at the Top* (Grinstead, Sussex: Eyre and Straker, 1962).

Breslow, L. and Buell, P., 'Mortality from coronary heart disease and physical activity of work in California', *J. Chron. Dis*, 11 (1960) 615–26.

Brook, A., 'Mental stress at work', *The Practitioner*, 210 (1973) 500–6.

Brooks, G. W. and Mueller, E. F., 'Serum urate concentrations among university professors', *J. Amer. Med. Assoc.*, 195 (1966) 415–18.

Brown, G. W., Sklair, F., Harris, T. O. and Birley, J. L. T., 'Life events and psychiatric disorders, Part I: Some methodological issues', *Psychological Medicine*, vol. 3, no. 1 (1973).

Brozek, J., Keys, A. and Blackburn, H., 'Personality differences between potential coronary and non-coronary patients', *Annals of New York Academy of Science*, 134 (1966) 1057–64.

Bruhn, J. G., Chandler, B. and Wolf, S., 'A psychological study of survivors and non-survivors of myocardial infarction', *Psychosom. Med.*, 31 (1969) 8–19.

Buck, V., *Working Under Pressure* (London: Staples Press, 1972).

Budner, S., 'Intolerance of ambiguity as a personality variable', *Journal of Personality*, 30 (1962).

Burns, L. E., 'Management of Stress'. A one week residential course organised by the University of Manchester, Extra-Mural Dept (July, 1976).

Burns, T. and Stalker, G. M., *The Management of Innovation* (London, The Tavistock, 1961).

Cannon, W. B., 'Stresses and strains of homeostasis', *Am. J. Med., Sci.*, 189, 1 (1935).

Caplan, G., *Principles of Preventive Psychiatry* (London: Tavistock, 1964).

Caplan, R. D., Cobb, S. and French, J. R. P., 'Relationships of cessation of smoking with job stress, personality and social support', *J. of Applied Psychology*, 60 (2) (1975) 211–19.

Caplan, R. D., Cobb, S., French, J. R. P., Van Harison, R. and Pinneau, S. R., 'Job demands and worker health: Main effects and occupational differences', *Niosh Research Report* (1975).

Caplan, R. D. and Jones, K. W., 'Effects of workload, role ambiguity and Type A personality on anxiety, depression and heart rate', *J. of Applied Psychology*, 60 (b) (1975) 713–19.

Carlestan, G., 'The individual, the city and stress', in L. Levi (ed.), *Society, Stress and Disease*, vol. 1 (London: Oxford University Press, 1971) p. 114–47.

Carruthers, M. E., 'Risk factor control'. Paper presented to the conference 'Stresses of the Air Traffic Control Officer (Latest Developments)' (Manchester, April, 1976).

Cattell, R. B., Eber, H. W. and Tatsuoka, M. M., *Handbook for the Sixteen Personality Factor Questionnaire (16PF)* (Windsor Books, NFER Publishing Co. Ltd., 1970).

Cattell, R. B., Rickets, K. Weise, C., Gray, B. and Yee, R., 'The effects of psychotherapy upon measured anxiety and aggression', *American Journal of Psychotherapy*, 20 (1966) 261–9.

Cattell, R. B. and Scheier, I. H., 'Stimuli related to stress, neuroticism, excitation and anxiety response patterns', *Journal of Abnormal and Social Psychology*, 60 (1960) 195–204.

Child, D., *The Essentials of Factor Analysis* (New York: Holt, Rinehart and Winston, 1970).

Christenson, W. S. and Hinkle, L. E., 'Differences in illness and prognostic signs in two groups of young men', *Journal of the American Medical Association*, 177 (1961) 247–53.

Clutterbuck, D., 'How I learned to stop worrying and love the job', *International Management*, 28 (8) (1973) 27–9.

Coch, L. and French, J. R. P., 'Overcoming resistance to change', *Hum. Relat.*, 11 (1948) 512–32.

Cofer, C. N. and Appley, M. H., *Motivation: Theory and Research* (New York: Wiley, 1964).

Comrey, A. L., *A First Course in Factor Analysis* (London: Academic Press, 1973).

Conley, R. W., Conwell, M. and Arill, M. B., 'An approach to measuring the cost of mental illness', in R. L. Noland (ed.), *Industrial Mental Health and Employee Counselling* (New York: Behavioural Publications, 1973).

Constandse, W. J., 'Mid-40s man: A neglected personnel problem', *Personnel Journal*, 51 (2) (1972) 129.

Cooper, C. L., *Group Training for Individual and Organisational Development* (Basel: Switzerland, S. Karger, 1973).

Cooper, C. L. and Mangham, I., *T-Groups: A Survey of Research* (London: Wiley, 1971).

Cooper, C. L. and Marshall, J., 'Stress and pressures within organisations, *Management Decison*, 13 (5) (1975a) 292–303.

Cooper, C. L. and Marshall, J., *Understanding Executive Stress* (London: Macmillan, 1978).

Cooper, C. L. and Marshall, J., 'The Management of stress', *Personnel Review*, 4 (4) (1975b).

Corneille, P., *Le Cid* (1666) in *Gem Dictionary of Quotations* (Collins).

Corson, S. A., 'Pavlovian and operant conditioning techniques in the study of psychosocial and biological relationships', in L. Levi (ed.), *Society, Stress and Disease*, vol. 1, 'The psychosocial environment and psychosomatic diseases (London: Oxford University Press, 1971) pp. 7–21.

Davis, L., 'Face the future with skill and enthusiasm', *The Times* (6 March 1975).

Dohrenwend, B. P., 'The social psychological nature of stress: A framework for causal inquiry', *Journal of Abnormal and Social Psychology* 62 (2) (1961) 294–302.

Dohrenwend, B. S. and Dohrenwend, B. P., *Stressful Life Events* (New York: Wiley 1974).

Donaldson, J. and Gowler, D., 'Perogatives, participation and managerial stress', in D. Gowler and K. Legge (eds.), *Managerial Stress* (Epping: Gower Press, 1975).

Doyle, C., 'Stress isn't such a killer after all' *Observer* (9 November, 1975).

Dreyfuss, F. and Czackes, J. W., 'Blood cholesterol and uric acid of healthy medical students under stress of examination', *Arch. Int. Med.,* 103 (1959) 798.

Eaton, M. T., 'The mental health of the older executive', *Geriat.,* 24 (1969) 126–34.

Epstein, S. and Fenz, W. D., 'Steepness of approach and avoidance gradients in humans as a function of experience: Theory and experiment', *Journal of Experimental Psychology,* 70 (1965) 1–12.

Erikson, E. H., *Identity and the life cycle*, Psychological Issues Monograph, vol. 1, no. 1 (1969).

Erikson, J., Edwards, D. and Gunderson, E. K., 'Status congruency and mental health', *Psychological Reports,* 33 (1973) 395–401.

Erikson, J., Pugh, W. M. and Gunderson, E. K., 'Status congruency as a predictor of job satisfaction and life stress,' *Journal of Applied Psychology,* 56 (1972) 523–5.

Eysenck, H. J., Arnold, W. J. and Meili, R. (eds.), *Encyclopedia of Psychology* (Bungay, Suffolk: Richard Clay (The Chaucer Press) Ltd., 1972).

Felton, J. S. and Cole, R., 'The high cost of heart disease', *Circulation,* 27 (1963) 957–2.

Fink, S. L., Beak, J. and Taddeo, K., 'Organisational crisis and change', *J. of Applied Behavioural Science,* 7 (1) (1971) 15–37.

Finn, F., Hickey, N. and O'Doherty, E. F., 'The psychological profiles of male and female patients with CHD, *Irish J. Med. Sci,* 2 (1969) 339–41.

Fisher, M., *The Executive* (London, New English Library, 1970).

Fogarty, M. P., Rapaport, R. and Rapaport, R., *Sex, Career and Family* (London: George Allen and Unwin, 1971).

French, J. R. P., 'Person–Role fit', *Occupational Mental Health,* 3(1) (1973).

French, J. R. P., and Caplan, R. D., 'Psychosocial factors in coronary heart disease', *Indus. Med.,* 39 (1970) 383–97.

French, J. R. P. and Caplan, R. D., 'Organisational stress and individual strain', in Marrow (ed.), *The Failure of Success* (New York: AMACOM, 1973), pp. 30–66.

French, J. R. P., Israel, J. and AS, D., 'An experiment in participation in a Norwegian factory, *Hum. Relat.,* 13 (1) (1960) 3–20.

French, J. R. P., Tupper, C. J., and Mueller, E. I., 'Workload of university professors' (Unpublished research report, Ann Arbor, Mich.: University of Michigan, 1965).

Friedman, M., *Pathogenesis of Coronary Artery Disease* (New York: McGraw Hill, 1969).

Friedman, M., Rosenman, R. H. and Carroll, V., 'Changes in serum cholesterol and blood clotting time in men subjected to cyclic variations of occupational stress', *Circulation,* 17 (1958) 852–61.

Froberg, J., Karlsson, C-G., Levi, L. and Lidberg, L., 'Physiological and biochemical stress reactions induced by psychosocial stimuli', in L. Levi (ed.), *Society, Stress and Disease,* vol. 1 (London: Oxford University Press, 1971) pp.

280–98.

Gemill, G. R. and Heisler, W. J., 'Machiavellianism as a factor in manageral job strain, job satisfaction and upward mobility', *Academy of Management J.*, 15 (1) (1972) 51–62.

Gillespie, F., 'Stress costs more than strikes', *Financial Times* (26 April, 1974).

Glaser, B. G. and Strauss, A. L., *The Discovery of Grounded Theory: Strategies for Qualitative Research* (London: Weidenfeld and Nicholson, 1967).

Glaser, B. G., and Strauss, A. L., *Status Passage* (London: Aldine, 1969).

Glass, A. J., 'Psychological aspects of emergency situations', in H. S. Abram (ed.), *Psychological aspects of stress* (Papers from a symposium held at Virginia Univ., Springfield, Ill: Thomas, 1970).

Goffman, E., 'On cooling the mark out', *Psychiatry*, 15 (4) (1952) 451–63.

Golembiewski, B. T. and McConkie, M., 'The Centrality of Interpersonal Trust', in C. L. Cooper (ed.), *Theories of Group Processes* (New York: Wiley, 1975).

Gowler, D. and Legge, K., 'Stress and external relationships – the "hidden contract",' in D. Gowler and K. Legge (eds.), *Managerial Stress* (Epping: Gower Press, 1975).

Guardian, The, ' Stress and the law' (29 July, 1974).

Guest, D. and Williams, R., 'How home affects work', *New Society* (18 January, 1973).

Gurin, G., Veroff, J. and Feld, S., *Americans View their Mental Health* (New York: Basic Books, 1960).

Hackman, J. R., 'Tasks and task performance in research on stress', in J. E. McGrath (ed.), *Social and Psychological Factors in Stress* (New York: Holt, Rinehart and Winston, 1970) pp. 202–37.

Handy, C., 'Difficulties of combining family and career', *The Times* (22 September, 1975) p. 16.

Hartston, W. R. and Mottram, R. D., *Personality Profiles of Managers: A study of occupational differences* (Cambridge: ITRU Publication SL9, 1975).

Heller, J., *Something happened* (New York: Ballantine Books, 1975).

Herzberg, F., *Work and the nature of man* (London: Staples Press, 1966).

Hinkle, L. E., 'The concept of "Stress" in the biological and social sciences', *Science, Medicine and Man*, 1 (1973) 31–48.

Hinkle, L. E., 'Effect of exposure to culture change, social change and changes in interpersonal relations on health', in B. S. Dohrenwald and B. P. Dohrenwald (eds.), *Stressful Life Events: Their Nature & Effects* (New York: Wiley, 1974) pp. 9–44.

Holmes, T. H. and Masuda, M., 'Life change and illness susceptibility', *Separation and Depression AAAS* (1973) 161–86.

Homes and Gardens, 'Stress' (August, 1974) pp. 53–60.

House, J., 'Northern managers on the move', *Management Decision* (Spring, 1969).

House, J. S., The effects of occupational stress on physical health', in J. O'Toole (ed.), *Work and the quality of life* (Cambridge, Mass: MIT Press, 1974).

Immundo, L. V., 'Problems associated with managerial mobility', *Personnel Journal* 53, 12 (1974) 910.

Indik, B., Seashore, S. E. and Slesinger, J., 'Demographic correlates of psychological strain', *J. of Abnormal and Sociol.* 4, 69 (1) (1964) 26–38.

IPAT Information Bulletin, No. 9, 'New prediction possibilities for vocational and educational counselling with the 16PF' (Illinois: IPAT, 1963).

Jackson, E. F., 'Status consistency and symptoms of stress', *American Sociological Review*, 27, 4 (1962) 469–80.

Janis, I. L., *Stress and Frustration* (New York: Harcourt, 1969).

Jenkins, C. D., 'Psychologic and social precursors of coronary disease', *New Eng. J. Med.*, 284 (5) (1971a) 244–55.

Jenkins, C. D., 'Psychologic and social precursors of coronary disease', *New Eng. J. Med.*, 284 (6) (1971b) 307–17.

Jennings, E. E., *The Mobile Manager: A Study of the New Generation of Top Executives* (New York: Appleton, 1967).

Kahn, R. L., 'Some propositions toward a researchable conceptualisation of stress', in J. E. McGrath (ed.); *Social and Psychological Factors in Stress* (New York: Holt, Rinehart and Winston, 1970) pp. 97–103.

Kahn, R. L., 'Conflict, ambiguity and overload: three elements in job stress', *Occupational Mental Health* 3 (1) (1973).

Kahn, R. L., Wolfe, D. M., Quinn, R. P., Snoek, J. E. and Rosenthal, R. A., *Organisational Stress* (New York: Wiley, 1964).

Kasl, S. V., 'Mental health and the work environment', *J. Occup. Med.*, 15 (6) (1973) 509–18.

Kasl, S. and Cobb, S., 'Effects of parental status incongruence and discrepancy in physical and mental health of adult offspring', *Journal of Personality and Social Psychology*, Monograph 7, Whole No. 642 (1967) 1–15.

Kay, E., 'Middle management', in J. O'Toole (ed.), *Work and the quality of life* (Cambridge, Mass: MIT Press, 1974).

Kearns, J. L., *Stress in industry* (London: Priory Press, 1973).

Kelley, T. L., 'Comments on Wilson and Worcesters', 'note on factor analysis', *Psychometrika*, 23 (1958) pp. 187–200.

Kellner, R. K and Sheffield, B. F., 'A self-rating scale of distress', *Psychological Medicine* 3 (1) (1973).

Kenton, L., 'Stress', *Unilever Magazine*, no. 9 (1974).

Kornhauser, A., *Mental Health of the Industrial Worker* (New York: Wiley, 1965).

Kreitman, N., 'Married couples admitted to mental hospital', *British J. of Psychiatry*, 114 (1969) 699–718.

Kritsikis, S. P., Heinemann, A. L., and Eitner, S., 'Die *angina pectoris* im aspekt ihrer korrelation mit biologischer disposition, psychologischen und soziologischen emflussfaktoren', *Deutsch Gasundh*, 23 (1968) 1878–85.

Lazarus, R. S., *Psychological stress and the coping process* (New York: McGraw-Hill, 1966).

Lazarus, R. S., 'Cognitive and personality factors underlying threat and coping', in M. H. Appley and R. Trumbull, *Psychological Stress* (New York: Appleton, 1967).

Lazarus, R. S., 'The concepts of stress and disease', in L. Levi (ed.), *Society, Stress and Disease,* vol. 1 (London: Oxford University Press, 1971) p. 53–60.

Leanderson, R. and Levi, L., 'A new approach to the experimental study of stuttering and stress', *Acta oto-laryng* (Stockh) 311, suppl. 224, (1967).

Lebovits, B. Z., Shekelle, R. B. and Ostfeld, A. M., 'Prospective and retrospective studies of CHD, *Psychosom. Med.*, 29 (1967) 265–72.

Leighton, D. C., Harding, J. S., Macklin, D. B., Macmillan, A. M. and Leighton, A. H., *The character of danger* (New York: Basic Books, 1963).

Levinson, H., 'Problems that worry our executives', in A. J. Marrow (ed.), *The failure of success* (New York: Amacon, 1973).

Levy, R., 'Relief of the executive headache?' *Duns*, 101 (March, 1973) 101.

Lipawski, Z. J., 'Psychosocial aspects of disease', *Annals of International Medicine*, 71, (1969) 1197–2006.

Love, A. E. H., *The Mathematical Theory of Elasticity*, 7–14 (New York: Dove Publications, 1944).

McDonough, J. R., Hames, C. G., Stulb, S. C. and Garrison, G. E., 'Coronary heart disease among Negroes and Whites in Evans County, Georgia', *J. of Chron. Dis.*, 18 (1965) 443–68.

McGhee, L. C., 'Psychological signs of executive emotional problems', *Industrial Medicine and Surgery*, 32 (5) (1963) 180–1.

McGrath, J. E. (ed.) *Social and Psychological Factors in Stress* (New York: Holt, Rinehart and Winston, 1970a).

McGrath, J. E., 'A conceptual formulation for research on stress', in J. E. McGrath (ed.), *Social and Psychological Factors in Stress* (New York: Holt, Rinehart and Winston, 1970b) pp. 10–21.

McGrath, J. E., 'Major substantive issues: Time, setting and the coping process', in J. E. McGrath (ed.) *Social and Psychological Factors in Stress* (New York: Holt, Rinehart and Winston, 1970c) pp. 22–40.

McLean, A. A., 'Job stress and the psychosocial pressures of change', *Personnel* (Jan-February 1976).

Macmillan, A. M., 'The health opinion survey: Technique for estimating the prevalence of psychoneurotic and related types of disorders in communities' *Psychological Reports*, 3 (1957) 325–9.

McMurray, R. N., 'Mental illness: Society's and industry's six billion dollar burden', in R. N. Noland (ed.), *Industrial Mental Health and Employee Counselling* (New York: Behavioural Publications, 1973a).

McMurray, R. N., 'The executive neurosis', in R. L. Noland (ed.), *Industrial Mental Health and Employee Counselling* (New York: Behavioural Publications, 1973b).

Marcson, S., *Automation, Alientation and Anomie* (New York: Harper and Row, 1970).

Margolis, B. L. and Kroes, W. H., 'Work and the health of man', in J. O'Toole (ed.), *Work and the Quality of Life* (Cambridge, Mass: MIT Press, 1974).

Marks, R. U., in 'Social stress and cardiovascular disease', *The Millbank Memorial Fund Quarterly*, Vol. XLV, no. 2 (1967) 51–107.

Marshall, J. and Cooper, C. L., *The mobile manager and his wife* (Bradford, MCB, 1976).

Marshall, J., 'Job pressures and satisfactions at managerial levels'. (Unpublished Ph.D. thesis, University of Manchester, 1977).

Mechanic, D., 'Discussion of studies relating changes and illness', in B. S. Dohrenwald and B. P. Dohrenwald (eds.), *Stressful Life Events: Their Nature and Effects* (New York: Wiley, 1974) pp. 87–98.

Mellinger, G. D., 'Interpersonal trust as a factor in communication', *Journal of Abnormal and Social Psychology*, vol. 52 (1956) 304–9.

Mettlin, C. and Woelfel, J., 'Interpersonal influence and symptoms of stress', *Journal of Health and Social Behaviour*, 15 (4) (1974) 311–19.

Miller, J. G., 'Information input overload and psychopathology', *Amer. J.*

Psychiat, 8 (1969) 116.

Mills, I. H., 'The disease of failure of coping', *The Practitioner,* 217 (1976) 529–38.

Minzberg, H., *The nature of managerial work* (New York: Harper and Row, 1973).

Mordkoff, A. M. and Rand, M. A., 'Personality and adaptation to coronary artery disease', *Journal of Consult Clinical Psychology,* 32 (1968) 648–53.

Morris, J., 'Job Rotation', *Journal of Business* (October, 1956) 268–73.

Morris, J., 'Managerial stress and "the cross of relationships" ' in D. Gowler and K. Legge (eds.), *Managerial Stress* (Epping: Gower Press, 1975).

Morris, J. N. *et al.,* 'Coronary heart disease and physical activity of work: II. Statement and testing of provisional hypothesis, *The Lancet,* 2 (1953) 1111–20.

Myers, J. K., Lindenthal, J. J., 'Life events and psychiatric impairment', *Journal of Nervous and Mental Disease,* 152 (1971) 149–57.

Myers, J. K., Lindenthal, J. J., Pepper, M. P. and Ostrander, D. R., 'Life events and mental status: a longitudinal study', *Journal of Health and Social Behaviour,* 13 (December, 1972) 398–406.

Neff, W. S., *Work and Human Behaviour* (New York: Atherton Press, 1968).

NFER, Test Information Bulletin TIS/05.02. *16PF Form C* (American 1956 Edition) 'British Norms: Male middle and senior managers' (Windsor, Berks: NFER Publishing Co, 1970).

Nichols, P., *Forget-Me-Not Lane* (London: Faber, 1971).

Nie, N. H., Bent, D. D. and Hull C. H., *Statistical Package for the Social Sciences* (New York: McGraw Hill, 1970).

Nobbs, D., *The Fall and Rise of Reginald Perrin* (Harmondsworth, Middx: Penguin Books, 1976).

Office of Health Economics, *Off Sick* Pamphlet No. 36 (London, 1971).

Oppenheim, A. N., *Questionnaire Design and Attitude Measurement* (London: Heinemann, 1966).

Orole, T. S. *et al., Mental Health in the Metropolis* (New York: McGraw-Hill, 1962).

Osler, W., 'The Lumleian lectures on *angina pectoris', Lancet,* (1910) 1, 696–700, 839–44, 974–77.

Ostfeld, A. M., Lebovits, B. Z. and Shekelle, R. B., 'A prospective study of the relationship between personality and CHD', *Journal of Chronic Diseases,* 17 (1964) 265–76.

Packard, V., *A Nation of Strangers* (New York: McKay, 1975).

Paffenbarger, R. S., Wolf, P. A. and Notkin, J., 'Chronic disease in former college students', *American Journal of Epidemiology,* 83 (1966) 314–28.

Pahl, J. M. and Pahl, R. E., *Managers and their Wives* (London: Allen Lane, 1971).

Parkes, C. M., 'Psycho-social Transitions', *Social Science and Medicine,* 5 (1971) 101–15.

Parsons, T., 'The kinship system of the contemporary United States', *American Anthropology,* 45 (1943) 22–38.

Paul, O. *et al.,* 'A longitudinal study of coronary heart disease', *Circulation,* 28 (1963) 20–31.

Payne, R., ' "A" type work for "A" type people?', *Personnel Management,* vol. 7 (1975) 22–4.

Pell, S. and D'Alonzo, C. A., 'Myocardial infarction in a one year industrial study', *Journal of the American Medical Association,* 166 (1958) 332–7.

Perham, J. C., 'Uptight executive', *Duns,* 99 (May, 1972) 79–80.

Pettigrew, A., 'Managing under Stress', *Management Today* (April, 1972).

Pickering, J. F., Harrison, J. A. and Cohen, C. D., 'Identification and measurement of consumer confidence: Methodology and some preliminary results', *Journal of the Royal Statistical Society*, 136 (1) (1973) 43–63.

Pierson, G. W., *The Moving American* (New York: Knopf, 1972).

Pincherle, G., *Fitness for work*. Proceedings of the Royal Society of Medicine, 65 (4) (1972) 321–4.

Porter, L. W. and Lawler, E. F., 'Properties of organisation structure in relation to job attitudes and job behaviour', *Psychological Bulletin*, 64 (1965) 23–51.

PROMSTRA, Discussion during seminar on 'Work Stress: Diagnosis and therapy', (September, 1976).

Quinlan, C. B., Burrow, J. G. and Hayes, C. G., 'The association of risk factors and CHD in Trappist and Benedictine monks'. Paper presented to the American Heart Association, New Orleans, Louisiana (1969).

Quinn, R. P., Seashore, S. and Mangione, I., *Survey of Working Conditions* (US Government Printing Office, 1971).

Rapoport, R. and Rapoport, R., 'New Light on the honeymoon', *Human Relations*, 17 (1964).

Reddin, W., *Managerial Effectiveness* (New York: McGraw-Hill, 1970).

Roche, G. R., 'Compensation and the mobile executive', *Harvard Business Review*, (November–December, 1975) 53–62.

Roget's *Thesaurus* (Aylesbury, Bucks: Penguin Books, 1966).

Rosenman, R. H., Friedman, M. and Jenkins, C. D., 'Clinically unrecognised myocardial infarction in the Western Collaborative Group Study', *American Journal of Cardiology*, 19 (1967) 776–82.

Rosenman, R. H., Friedman, M. and Strauss, R., 'A predictive study of CHD', *Journal of the American Medical Association*, 189 (1964) 15–22.

Rosenman, R. H., Friedman, M. and Strauss, R., 'CHD in the Western Collaborative Group Study', *Journal of the American Medical Association*, 195 (1966) 86–92.

Rummel, R. J., *Applied Factor Analysis* (Evanston: Northwestern University Press, 1970).

Russek, H. I. and Zohman, B. L., 'Relative significance of hereditary, diet and occupational stress in CHD of young adults', *American Journal of Medical Science*, 235 (1958) 266–5.

Ryle, J. A. and Russell, W. T., 'The natural history of coronary disease: A clinical and epidemiological study', *British Heart Journal*, 11 (1949) 370–89.

Sales, S. M., 'Differences among individuals in affective, behavioural, biochemical, and physiological responses to variations in work load'. Doctoral Dissertation The University of Michigan, Ann Arbor, Mich: University Microfilms no. 60–18098 (1969).

Sartre, J. P., *Huis Clos* (Paris: Theatre Gallimard, 1947).

Seidenberg, R., 'Corporate wives – corporate casualties', *American Management* (1973).

Selye, H., 'The general adaptation syndrome and the diseases of adaptation', *Journal of Clinical Endocrinology*, 6, 117 (1946).

Shekelle, R. B., Ostfeld, A. M. and Paul, O., 'Social status and incidence of CHD', *Journal of Diseases*, 22 (1969) 381–94.

Shepard, J. M., *Automation and Alienation* (Cambridge, Mass: MIT Press, 1971).

Shirom, A., Eden, D., Silberwasser, S. and Kellerman, J. J., 'Job stresses and risk factors in coronary heart disease among occupational categories in kibbutzim', *Social Science and Medicine* 7 (1973) 875–92.

Shorter Oxford English Dictionary. Revised and edited by C. T. Onions (Oxford: Clarendon Press, 1933).

Shostrom, E. L., *Personal Orientation Inventory.* Educational and Industrial Testing service (San Diego, California, 1962).

Sleeper, R. D., 'Labour mobility over the life cycle', *British Journal of Industrial Relations,* XIII, 2 (1975).

Smith, J., 'Can companies reduce executive heart attacks?' *Duns,* 95 (April, 1970) 51–2.

Smith, T., 'Sociocultural incongruity and change: A review of empirical findings', in S. L. Syme and L. G. Reeder (eds.), *Social Stress and Cardiovascular Disease,* Millbank Memorial Foundation Quarterly, vol. XLV, no. 2, part 2 (1967).

Sofer, C., *Men in Mid-Career* (Cambridge University Press, 1970).

Spain, D. M., 'Problems in the study of coronary atherosclerosis in population groups in culture, society and health', *Annals of the New York Academy Sciences,* 84 (1960) 816–34.

Srole, L., Langner, T. S., Michael, S. T., Opler, M. K. and Rennie, A. C., *Mental Health in the Metropolis: The Midtown Manhattan Study* (New York: McGraw Hill, 1962).

Stamler, J., Kjelisberg, M. and Hall, Y., 'Epidemiologic studies of cardiovascular-renal diseases: I. Analysis of mortality by age, race, sex and occupation', *Journal of Chronic Diseases,* 12 (1960) 440–55.

Steiner, I. D., 'Strategies for controlling stress in interpersonal situations', in J. E. McGrath (ed.), *Social and Psychological Factors in stress* (New York: Holt, Rinehart and Winston, 1970) 140–58.

Stouffer, S. A., Guttman, L., Suchman, E. A., Lazarsfeld, P. F., Starr, S. A. and Claussen, J. A., *Measurement and prediction: Studies in social psychology in World War II* (Princeton: Princeton University Press, 1950).

Sunday Times, The 'Life Span, Stress' (15 February, 1976) 14–15.

Syme, S. L., Borhani, N. O. and Beuchley, R. W., 'Cultural mobility and coronary heart disease in the urban area', *American Journal of Epidemiology,* 82 (1965) 334–46.

Syme, S. L. Hyman, M. M. and Enterline, P. E., 'Some social and cultural factors associated with the occurrence of coronary heart disease', *Journal of Chronic Diseases,* 17 (1964) 277–89.

Syme, S. L., Hyman, M. M. and Enterline, P. E., 'Cultural mobility and the occurrence of coronary heart disease', *Journal of Health and Human Behaviour,* 6, (1965) 178–89.

Taylor, G. R., *Rethink* (London: Secker and Warburg, 1972).

Taylor, R., 'Stress at Work', *New Society* (17 October, 1974).

Terhure, W. B., 'Emotional problems of executives in time', *Industrial Med. Surg.,* 32 (1963) 1–67.

Terryberry, S., 'The organisation of environments'. (Unpublished Ph.D. Thesis, Ann Arbor, Mich. University Microfilms (1968).)

Thomas, C. B. and Ross, D. C., 'Observations of some possible precursors of essential hypertension and coronary heart disease in Social Stress and Cardiovascular, *Millbank Memorial Fund Qtrly.,* vol. XLV, no. 2 (1967).

Times, The, 'Reference to middle-class housing estate study' by Dr E. G. Cohen, Civil Service College (29 August, 1975).

Toffler, A., *Future Shock* (New York: Random, 1970).

Uris, A., 'How managers ease job pressures', *International Management* (27 June, 1972) 45–6.

Van Harrison, R., 'Job stress and worker health: person–environment misfit'. Paper presented at the *103rd Annual Meeting of the American Public Health Association* (Chicago, Illinois, 1975).

Vickers, R., 'A short measure of the Type A personality', *ISR Newsletter* (Michigan, Febuary, 1973).

Wagstaff, A. E., 'The dilemma of the middle-aged controller', Paper presented to the conference *Stresses of the Air Traffic Controller Officer (Latest Developments)* (Manchester, April, 1976).

Wardwell, W. I., Hyman, M. and Bahnson, C. B., 'Stress and coronary disease in three field studies', *Journal of Chronic Diseases,* 17 (1964) 73–84.

Warr, P. B. and Routledge, T., 'An opinion scale for the study of managers' job satisfaction', *Occupational Psychology,* 43 (1969) 95–109.

Webber, R. A., 'The roots of organisational stress', *Personnel,* 43 (5) (1966).

Weick, K. E., 'The "ess" in stress: Some conceptual and methodological problems', in J. E. McGrath (ed.), *Social and Psychological Factors in Stress* (New York: Holt, Rinehart and Winston, 1970) pp. 287–347.

Whorf, B. L., *Language, thought and reality* (New York: Wiley, 1956).

Wilson, S., *The Man in the Grey Flannel Suit* (New York: Rentloy (Reprint), 1972).

Wind, Y., A reward-balance model of buying behaviour', in G. Fisk (ed.), *New Essays in Marketing Theory* (Boston, USA: Allyn and Bacon Inc, 1971).

Wing, J. K., Birley, J. T. L., Cooper, J. E., Graham, P. and Isaacs, A. B., 'Procedure for measuring and classifying "present psychiatric state"' *British Journal of Psychiatry,* 113 (1966) 499–515.

Wolff, H. G., *Stress and Disease,* Springfield, Ill: C. C. Thomas, 1953).

Wolff, H. G. and Goodell, H., *Stress and Disease,* 2nd edn. Springfield, Ill; (C. C. Thomas, 1968).

Wright, H. B., 'Institute of Directors medical centre in London', in A. A. McLean (ed.), *To Work is Human: mental health and the business community* (New York: Rand, 1967).

Wright, H. B., Health hazards for executives', *Journal of General Management,* 2 (2) (1975a).

Wright, H. B., *Executive ease and dis-ease* (Epping: Gower Press, 1975b).

Wyler, A. R., Masuda, M. and Holmes, T. H., 'Magnitude of life events and seriousness of illness', *Psychosomatic Medicine,* vol. 33 (1971) 115–22.

Zuckerman, M., Levine, S. and Biase, D. V., 'Stress response in total and partial perceptual isolation, *Psychosomatic Medicine* 26 (3) (1964) 250–60.

Zyzanski, S. J. and Jenkins, C. D., 'Basic dimension within the coronary-prone behaviour pattern', *Journal of Chronic Diseases,* 22 (1970) 781–95.

Appendix I

DOING RESEARCH ON MANAGERIAL STRESS: THE PROBLEMS

Whilst both quantitative and qualitative data was collected in this study the systematic analysis of results relies heavily on the former. It is important here therefore to consider the principal merits and demerits of the tools used for its data collection and statistical analysis. The first three sections of this discussion of methodological issues thus cover the measures used as criteria of stress, the use of correlational analysis techniques and the Job Characteristics Questionnaire designed specifically for this study. Section 4 considers more general 'ethical' problems of research in this sensitive area. Finally in section 5 some suggestions for further research are put forward.

1. THE MEASURES USED AS CRITERIA OF STRESS

The study relied on subjective symptom-oriented rather than objective disease-based criteria measures of stress. Two distinctions are involved here: that between central and peripheral symptoms of stress and that between subject- and observer-rated variables. These will be discussed in turn.

The ultimate manifestations of stress are cardiovascular heart disease and mental 'breakdown' and the nearer one can as a researcher come to using these as dependent variables the more confidently one can draw conclusions from the data (other things being equal). In this case such information was not available: the company held only incomplete medical records for the sample and inclusion of a medical examination as part of the study was not practicable within the contract with them (which emphasised causing as little 'disruption' as possible). There is at present a fear of 'frank' research in the stress area which means that it is likely to be some time before such direct techniques for measuring stress are widely acceptable. (Hopefully norms on this issue will change as the benefits of the use of 'indisputable' illness measures becomes apparent.) The more remote the symptoms studied are from those 'absolute' indices the greater the likelihood that they are affected by factors other than supposedly causative stress and the more qualified conclusions based on them must be. The 16PF anxiety scale has been sufficiently validated and its relationship to associated emotional health measures well-established to escape major criticisms on this issue. Although the Gurin Psychosomatic Symptom List is not as sufficiently rigorously based conceptually as the 16PF it is still a fairly reliable and valid instrument.

Nevertheless the development of a better physical stress measure along similar lines (i.e. that can be administered as a self-completion paper-and-pencil test) should be a priority of those working in this area. An important first step would be to achieve an agreed medical definition of stress described in symptom as well as 'extreme illness' terms. This could be done experimentally by using medical diagnosis of more clear-cut indicators (e.g. blood pressure, serum cholesterol levels) as criteria against which to validate a new symptom check list. (Researchers have tended to rely on one or the other method of defining stress and have paid little attention to establishing the relationship between them.) A comprehensive pool of questionnaire items is already available in the literature and could be extended by discussion with medical prac-titioners especially those working in industry. An important part in such a development would be the investigation of whether derivation of a global (ill)-health score or scores on several distinguishable dimensions is the more valid. Factor analysis, a statistical technique of identifying inherent patterns in sets of responses, could be used to isolate sub-scales. (Another way of approaching the problem of adequately catering for individuals' distinct stress profiles, but one which is more open to 'faking', would be to calculate a respondent's score based only on those items he defines as being characteristic of stress for him.) Bearing in mind individual differences in stress responses it is perhaps unrealistic to attempt to develop one test suitable for all population segments. The managers in the sample appeared to be 'affronted' by the more femininely-biased items (especially 'crying easily') on the Gurin scale and development of at least separate male and female versions would in-tuitively appear to have both practical and conceptual benefits.

In this study the fact that symptoms were scored by subjects themselves rather than objective observers is a further potential problem. Such a method is open not only to conscious distortion (by 'faking') but also unconscious distortion if the respondent is unaware of (does not admit even to himself?) the symptoms he suffers. Whilst these possibilities must be borne in mind it does appear:

a. that in this study respondents were motivated to reply relatively frankly to the questionnaires used:
   i. motivational distortion scores on the 16PF were below the norm

ii. personality differences played no consistent part in determining the number of job pressures and satisfactions reported
and

iii. relatively high numbers of symptoms were reported on the
Gurin Psychosomatic Symptom List

b. that the need for self-awareness was minimised by the 'convert'
nature of the two scales; the anxiety scale was 'hidden' beneath the
first stratum personality items and the health scale asked for
ratings of objective, if somewhat threatening, behaviours. The
problem of 'distortion' can be avoided altogether by measuring
stress by medical examination or by looking to sources external to
the individual for dependent measures. Organisational
manifestations of stress – high labour turnover, poor staff
relations – are particularly relevant to a work-based study. In
situations where colleagues' and spouses' ratings of focal subjects
(e.g. managers) can be elicited, behavioural signs too can be used
as measures. These will be of two classes: the manifestations of
stress – feeling tired easily, an inability to relax and focusing on
short-term consequences for example – and indications of
attempts to cope with stress – working long hours, withdrawal,
apathy, excessive smoking or drinking.

From the wide range of measures available along these two dimensions the researcher must choose those appropriate to his particular
research context. Whilst this study can be criticised for failing to include
more objective stress measures this omission can be defended on both
practical (by choosing on 'acceptable' methodology access was gained to
an otherwise inaccessible population) and conceptual grounds (it was
consistent with the psychological approach to stress definition on which
the research design was based). The scales eventually used do also have
the benefit of having acquired considerable pragmatic 'respectability'
from their inclusion as stress measures in a wide range of studies. .

2. THE COLLECTION OF DATA AT ONE POINT IN, RATHER THAN OVER, TIME
AND ITS ANALYSIS BY CORRELATIONAL STATISTICAL TECHNIQUES

Stress as a state is a result of the interaction of an individual with his environment, over time. The research approach adopted here – the collection of data 'latitudinally' (i.e. from a relatively large sample, in broad
terms, at one point in time) rather than longitudinally (i.e. from a small
group in detail, over time) and its analysis by correlational
techniques – means that whilst we can identify elements in this
relationship we can come to only tentative conclusions about their
sequence of occurrence. The results of both the factor analysis and multiple regression stages of analysis are limited in the contribution they

can make to our understanding of the temporal aspects of stress.

Factor analysis revealed the dimensions along which this group of managers assessed their jobs; it could not indicate however whether certain derived job and organisational factors precede others in time (faith in the company is likely to be affected for example by changes in other pressures and satisfactions) or whether each is acute, chronic or recurring in its action (either for the population as a whole or for specific individuals). In considering (conceptually) the generality of results and (practically) priorities for attention the latter distinction is extremely important. An acute pressure is one which acts suddenly – relocation of the individual or new legislation at the aggregate level for example – and is usually overcome in time. Any pressure which operates all the time can be termed chronic; it should be a priority for attention but is likely to be more firmly rooted than others and therefore more resistant to change. A recurring pressure should also be a priority for concern especially if it is due to a past failure to adapt (the manager who *always* finds delegating a problem) rather than to an inevitable and possibly acceptable part of the job (the accountant's year-end deadlines).

The results from multiple regression analyses too are non-sequential. Our findings show only that particular variables are associated with high scores on the stress criteria measures but not whether the former are causes, additional symptoms or outcomes of stress. If in fact we bear in mind that symptoms and outcomes of stress can 'feed back' into the spiral and in their turn become causes it is perhaps unrealistic to expect that any statistical technique (even those to which longitudinal data is available) is capable of adequately depicting sequence in the stress reaction. This study compensated for this limitation in two ways; firstly by using multi-factorial techniques to arrive at interactive patterns of stress-related variables (rather than trying to depict complex situations in terms of relations between pairs of elements) and secondly by basing the interpretations of sequence within these patterns on interview accounts of the development of stress. The conclusion that 'seeking satisfaction outside work' was a contributory cause of work stress for one function (research) but a reaction to decreased job satisfaction for another (engineering) was for example suggested by interview data.

Despite its limitations correlational analysis is a powerful tool for the social scientist interested in understanding complex events. In this study it particularly provided the opportunity of looking at the full range of the samples' stress scores and finding out what other variables were associated with the distribution of this range. This approach has two important practical advantages over the alternative method of isolating groups of 'stressed' and 'unstressed' individuals for comparative analysis:

i. all of the sample can be retained for consideration (rather than excluding the middle 50% on the criterion distribution)
ii. it avoids the need to make premature assumptions about the data – in this case it would have been necessary to choose either one or the other or a compromise between the two criteria stress measures on which scores did not completely overlap.

It is also consistent (as it involved treating the sample *as a whole*) with the research aim of developing a comprehensive view of job pressures and satisfactions within which individuals or meaningful sub-groups could later be located. In this context factor analysis was a more immediately useful statistical technique than was multiple regression. The job factors which make up the aggregate framework derived from the former are ideal as standards against which variations within the sample can be investigated. We find by using such an approach that for these managers job satisfactions change over the life cycle – satisfaction from 'conflict' decreasing and that from 'relationships at work' increasing with age. In contrast the results from sample-wide multiple regression are not similarly useful; the aggregate profile of 'the manager at risk' is so broadly painted as to be misleading and cautions against making sweeping generalisations about 'the causes of stress'. An overview of risk factors can in fact only be achieved by comparing and contrasting meaningful population sub-groups.

This research approach has therefore limitations as well as considerable advantages. Consistency, both within and between, sets of findings does however go a long way towards compensating for such inadequacies. In this case both interview and literature material (but particularly the former) made an invaluable contribution to the interpretation and confirmation of questionnaire replies.

3. THE JOB AND ORGANISATIONAL CHARACTERISTICS QUESTIONNAIRE

Managers' satisfaction with the format and content of the Job Characteristics Questionnaire suggests that this scale had largely achieved its main structural aim of allowing individuals in a wide variety of circumstances adequate opportunities for self-expression. In retrospect two criticisms can however be made:

a. The final version contained only two items which dealt directly with the work:home interface. Interview data suggests that the following main dimensions should be covered by additional items to correct this deficiency:

the manager's wife's attitude to his work – whether she is supportive or resents its domination of home life whether there is pressure on him from home to spend more time with his family or participate more in running the house (especially if he has a working wife)

the manager's ability to segregate work and home activities (or to amalgamate the two successfully)

his ability to 'switch off' in the evenings and at weekends and pursue satisfying outside interests.

b. Respondents were given no opportunity to rate their pressure from and satisfaction with 'work as a whole' and with broad job dimensions. The addition of such scales would benefit both respondents and researchers; the former by having an opportunity to give his overall balanced assessment and the latter by eliciting global standards against which responses to individual items could be judged. The scale will therefore be extended for future use to include overall scales – one for 'work life as a whole' and several to cover major job dimensions. Choice of these dimensions is at the moment problematic as two similar but conflicting frameworks are available: the first, that of the headings under which potential stresses from the literature review and interview data were grouped; and the second, the job factors derived by factor analysis. Conceptually the latter is preferable as these appear to be the dimensions on which respondents judged their jobs; it is however sample- and study-specific and its relevance to other, even similar, populations has still to be established. As a provisional measure a synthesis of the two frameworks along the following lines is suggested:

Job as a whole
Workload
Challenges in the job
Opportunities for independence/autonomy
Relationships
Managing people
Career progress
Extent to which your contribution is appreciated
Job security
Working for the company
Balance between work and home lives

The Job and Organisational Characteristics Questionnaire proved a good tool with which to investigate both practical and conceptual issues. In its present form it is probably limited to use with managerial populations similar to that studied but could be easily modified (based on interview data) for use with other occupational groups. Taken together the questionnaire, factor analysis and multiple regression analysis offer a 'compact' methodology for investigating job pressures and satisfactions in a wide range of contexts.

4. METHODOLOGICAL AND ETHICAL IMPLICATIONS OF RESEARCH AS AN INTERVENTION

One of the less obvious advantages of 'latitudinal' over 'longitudinal' studies is that the former can be achieved with the minimum of interference in the respondents' life. This has both methodological and ethical implications. A major concern of social scientists in any area is that their 'intervention' will have some effect on the mental process, behaviour etc. which they want to study and that they will not therefore obtain a 'true reading'. This is a particularly crucial problem in longitudinal research on stress: the initial contact, whether by questionnaire or interview, is likely to sensitise the individual to the topic and affect this future perception of, coping with, and perhaps even tolerance for, stress. The ultimate outcome for the subject may be either harmful or beneficial; it will however almost certainly be beyond the knowledge and the control of the researcher. Evidence of the powerful nature of such an effect came from the small sample interviewed. For some intervention was an impetus to constructive planning, others found that being made to think in detail about the mechanics and psychosocial implications of moving made them more vulnerable especially to those pressures outside their control.

This is not merely a methodological problem of obtaining distorted results; it is one of the ethics of interfering in individuals' lives. The data-distortion consequences of a 'one-point-in-time' study such as this one were kept to a minimum, but the researchers cannot absolve themselves from all responsibility for the future consequences of their intervention. The data-collection approach adopted in this study – official approval from the company doctor, an emphasis on confidentiality, return of the bulk of correspondence directly to the university and personal or telephone contact wherever possible – helped to reduce respondents' 'anxiety-due-to-participation'. A more explicit approach on such an emotive topic is not however advised unless adequate provision can be made for assessing and coping with the effect on respondents of the researcher's intrusion.

In longitudinal research it would we feel be both necessary and desirable to combine research with individual counselling. (In several interviews in fact the researchers felt the need to adopt a counselling role to cope with the anxieties discussion of the topic had raised.) This would have not only ethical but also methodological advantages:

    i. one can reap the benefits of *known* intervention. Results will be different from those collected by a completely unobtrusive observer (an unrealistic although common ideal in such a field)

ii. data on causes of stress, coping, possible action and their outcomes will all be covered in one research study and on the same population

iii. it would be possible to elicit much franker data by actively involving the respondent in the research process. Researchers would then gain access to the 'ultimate' subjective as well as objective criteria of stress.

The third advantage is particularly important. In present circumstances a variety of mechanisms appear to be operating to prevent subjects reporting stress symptoms 'accurately'; chief of these are:

lack of self-awareness

preference for the socially desirable response

lack of faith in the confidentiality of research data.

Only the development of a long-term, non-threatening, even supportive, relationship between researcher and respondent can fully justify breaching (even unknowingly) the latter's defences in any way. The findings reported here suggest that this is a potentially acceptable research methodology even in such a 'sensitive' area. The high questionnaire response rate of 89% (Oppenheim (1966) says of self-completion questionnaire response rates that 'even in studies of interested groups, 80% is seldom exceeded') suggests that stress is a topic of considerable relevance to this sample and one which they are prepared to 'discuss' given appropriate circumstances.

5. SUGGESTIONS FOR FUTURE RESEARCH

Whilst many of the research findings are study- and company-specific results do have a certain validity outside this particular organisation. Both methodology and conceptual implications can be easily transferred to other settings. Some content too will be relevant 'outside'. We can expect the concerns and satisfactions expressed to be applicable to managers in a wide range of organisations although not in the same relative strengths. The profiles of individuals 'at risk' are also likely to have meaning wherever job demands and managers' personality characteristics are similar to those found here.

In order to compare these groups meaningfully the research design will need to be expanded to include some measurement of organisational variables. Understanding of the impact of company-size, technology (particularly whether it is a fast-changing or stable industry), structure and atmosphere on managerial stress can make not only an important conceptual contribution but help to guide strategies for the latter's control.

Further research 'vertically' as well as 'horizontally' is needed to put these findings in context. As with any piece of social psychological research which isolates and studies only part of an individual it has touched on 'neighbouring areas' which have direct bearing on the focus topics but which, for practical reasons (limitations on data collection and conceptual manipulation capabilities), it was not possible to cover in-depth. Each of these areas is in itself a possible overlapping research project. Those of direct relevance to our study can be grouped under three headings: the individual, the working environment and home life. *The individual's* self-awareness, motivations and aspirations (and how these change) are important determinants of his approach to and expectations of work. These not only change with age but also in response to changing conditions in the world outside. Our current economic crisis (the last and 'best' in a 30-year downhill slide) has had effects on morale and expectations at all levels of the work force and has resulted in even economists recognising 'attitudes' as respectable variables (e.g. Pickering, Harrison and Cohen, 1973). Researchers must therefore look more closely at worker attitudes especially in the area of stress where they play such an important mediating role.

In the context of the *sample company* this study is only a first step in a more lengthy process of examining the *status quo* and planning action for its future improvement. By identifying job pressures and satisfaction it has pointed to 'areas of need' but this is no more than a preliminary basis from which remedies can be suggested. Research could also be used to generate ideas as to what actions are appropriate and by whom these should be undertaken. For such a study the sample needs to be broadened to include company representatives as well as employee managers so that both individual job satisfaction and company performance interests will be adequately represented. If these two 'sides' can in fact discuss and negotiate such issues together solutions to which both are committed can be agreed. Another pre-condition to effective action is an awareness of (and willingness to change if necessary) company norms and values. These determine individual employees' attitudes to experiencing, revealing and managing stress and currently appear to be acting (not only in this organisation but in 'society' as a whole) to deter adaptive coping in certain contexts.

The relationship between work stress and *home life* in particular deserves more systematic investigation than it received here. The two most important dimensions, as far as the manager in his work role is concerned, appear to be those of time management and social support. Factors such as the wife's 'occupation', her satisfaction with this, the part the manager's job plays in their joint life, the extent to which he is required and wants to participate in activities outside work all have significant bearing on these and ultimately the manager's 'performance' in his job. Their investigation is of considerable topical interest and should be carried out with continual reference to changes in society's values and practices.

Appendix 2

JOB CHARACTERISTICS QUESTIONNAIRE

The aim of this questionnaire is to see how people feel about the multitude of components which go to make up their overall job situation. By using factor analysis I hope to be able to examine what clusters of pressures and satisfactions go together and thus to throw some light on the way in which job factors interact with each other and with the characteristics of the individual doing the job.

Remember Do not spend time pondering. You will find completion easiest if you do it fairly swiftly.

SECTION A

Below are a series of statements about possible job situations. For each one that applies to you please indicate to what extent it is a source of pressure or a source of satisfaction by *circling the appropriate code*. If an item is a source of both pressure and satisfaction please show this by circling two codes.

If a statement does not apply or is untrue please circle NA for Not Applicable.

Definitions

Pressure = a problem, something you find difficult to cope with, about which you feel worried or anxious.

Satisfaction = something you enjoy which contributes to your sense of achievement, etc.

Codes

5 = a source of *extreme* pressure or satisfaction.
3 = a source of *moderate* pressure or satisfaction.
1 = a source of *slight* pressure or satisfaction.
0 = *neither* a source of pressure nor a source of satisfaction.

		Pressure		Satisfaction
1.	My position requires that I make a lot of important decisions.	5 4 3 2 1	0	1 2 3 4 5 NA
2.	I seldom know what higher management expects of me.	5 4 3 2 1	0	1 2 3 4 5 NA
3.	I spend a lot of time dealing with 'people-problems'.	5 4 3 2 1	0	1 2 3 4 5 NA
4.	If I make mistakes in my job my career is likely to suffer.	5 4 3 2 1	0	1 2 3 4 5 NA
5.	Standards don't stand still here; I'm always expected to perform better than I did the last time.	5 4 3 2 1	0	1 2 3 4 5 NA
6.	I feel like a small cog in a big machine.	5 4 3 2 1	0	1 2 3 4 5 NA
7.	This company is quick to adopt new ideas.	5 4 3 2 1	0	1 2 3 4 5 NA
8.	In doing my job I get very little support from higher management.	5 4 3 2 1	0	1 2 3 4 5 NA
9.	I frequently find that my beliefs conflict with those of the company.	5 4 3 2 1	0	1 2 3 4 5 NA
10.	In a large company like this it is not always easy to find out what is going on.	5 4 3 2 1	0	1 2 3 4 5 NA
11.	I sometimes feel that I am trapped by the system here.	5 4 3 2 1	0	1 2 3 4 5 NA
12.	My opinions are usually considered when decisions are made.	5 4 3 2 1	0	1 2 3 4 5 NA
13.	I am constantly asked to use new methods and deal with new problems.	5 4 3 2 1	0	1 2 3 4 5 NA
14.	I sometimes find myself caught between two groups with conflicting interests.	5 4 3 2 1	0	1 2 3 4 5 NA
15.	It seems likely that I shall stay with this company until I retire.	5 4 3 2 1	0	1 2 3 4 5 NA
16.	I feel that working for this company imposes restrictions on my behaviour.	5 4 3 2 1	0	1 2 3 4 5 NA
17.	If I make mistakes in my job there could be serious consequences for the company.	5 4 3 2 1	0	1 2 3 4 5 NA
18.	This company is slow to react to new situations.	5 4 3 2 1	0	1 2 3 4 5 NA
		Pressure		*Satisfaction*

	Pressure		Satisfaction

19. I think it likely I shall be asked
    to retire early. 5 4 3 2 1   o   1 2 3 4 5 NA
20. I sometimes have to work long
    hours and/or take work home to
    get things done. 5 4 3 2 1   o   1 2 3 4 5 NA
21. I sometimes find myself passing
    on orders I don't agree with. 5 4 3 2 1   o   1 2 3 4 5 NA
22. I have probably reached my career
    ceiling. 5 4 3 2 1   o   1 2 3 4 5 NA
23. Later in my career I might well be
    asked to change to a completely
    different type of work. 5 4 3 2 1   o   1 2 3 4 5 NA
24. I am often faced with a choice
    between family and work demands. 5 4 3 2 1   o   1 2 3 4 5 NA
25. I do not have to take many
    decisions on my own. 5 4 3 2 1   o   1 2 3 4 5 NA
    Pressure   *Satisfaction*

SECTION B

You are asked not to complete the sentence. Just indicate to what extent each job factor is a source of pressure or satisfaction by circling appropriately.

| | *Pressure* | | *Satisfaction* |

1. My physical working conditions are ... 5 4 3 2 1   o   1 2 3 4 5 NA
2. The time pressures and deadlines in
   my job are ... 5 4 3 2 1   o   1 2 3 4 5 NA
3. I find managing people ... 5 4 3 2 1   o   1 2 3 4 5 NA
4. My contacts with people in other
   departments are ... 5 4 3 2 1   o   1 2 3 4 5 NA
5. My rate of promotion is ... 5 4 3 2 1   o   1 2 3 4 5 NA
6. On the whole the content of the job
   I do is ... 5 4 3 2 1   o   1 2 3 4 5 NA
7. My relationships with work
   colleagues are ... 5 4 3 2 1   o   1 2 3 4 5 NA
8. Keeping up with developments in
   my field is ... 5 4 3 2 1   o   1 2 3 4 5 NA
9. My job prospects outside the company
   are ... 5 4 3 2 1   o   1 2 3 4 5 NA
10. Spending 'leisure' time on work
    rather than other things is ... 5 4 3 2 1   o   1 2 3 4 5 NA
11. My relationship with my superior is ... 5 4 3 2 1   o   1 2 3 4 5 NA
12. The likelihood that I would lose
    my job through staff cutbacks is ... 5 4 3 2 1   o   1 2 3 4 5 NA

	Pressure		Satisfaction
13. Personality conflicts at work are . . .	5 4 3 2 1	0	1 2 3 4 5 NA
14. Planning work and setting priorities is . . .	5 4 3 2 1	0	1 2 3 4 5 NA
15. The rules and regulations of a company this size are . . .	5 4 3 2 1	0	1 2 3 4 5 NA
16. My contacts with people outside the company are . . .	5 4 3 2 1	0	1 2 3 4 5 NA
17. I find office politics . . .	5 4 3 2 1	0	1 2 3 4 5 NA
18. My promotion prospects in this company are . . .	5 4 3 2 1	0	1 2 3 4 5 NA
19. My relationships with subordinates are . . .	5 4 3 2 1	0	1 2 3 4 5 NA
20. My rate of pay is . . .	5 4 3 2 1	0	1 2 3 4 5 NA
21. I find delegating authority . . .	5 4 3 2 1	0	1 2 3 4 5 NA
22. The travelling involved in my job is . . .	5 4 3 2 1	0	1 2 3 4 5 NA
	Pressure		*Satisfaction*

SECTION C

In this section each item covers two possible circumstances only one of which is likely to apply to you.

First please indicate which statement (if any) applies by marking the appropriate box and *then* go on to indicate whether this is a source of pressure or satisfaction.

		Pressure		Satisfaction
1a. This job is comfortably within my capabilities.	☐	5 4 3 2 1	0	1 2 3 4 5 NA
b. This job stretches me to the limit of my capabilities.	☐	5 4 3 2 1	0	1 2 3 4 5 NA
2a. I have *a lot of* responsibility for money and equipment.	☐	5 4 3 2 1	0	1 2 3 4 5 NA
b. I have *very little* responsibility for money and equipment	☐	5 4 3 2 1	0	1 2 3 4 5 NA
3a. I have more work than I can adequately cope with.	☐	5 4 3 2 1	0	1 2 3 4 5 NA
b. It is difficult to find enough work to fill the day.	☐	5 4 3 2 1	0	1 2 3 4 5 NA
4a. I can discuss *very few* work problems with fellow managers.	☐	5 4 3 2 1	0	1 2 3 4 5 NA
b. I can discuss *most* work problems with fellow managers.	☐	5 4 3 2 1	0	1 2 3 4 5 NA
5a. The work I do is *usually* recognised and appreciated.	☐	5 4 3 2 1	0	1 2 3 4 5 NA
		Pressure		*Satisfaction*

	Pressure		Satisfaction

b. The work I do is *seldom* recognised
and appreciated. □ 5 4 3 2 1   0   1 2 3 4 5 NA

6a. There is a *lot of* communication
and consultation in this
company □ 5 4 3 2 1   0   1 2 3 4 5 NA

b. There is *little* communication
and consultation in this
company. □ 5 4 3 2 1   0   1 2 3 4 5 NA

7a. My superior *seldom* becomes
involved in the job I do. □ 5 4 3 2 1   0   1 2 3 4 5 NA

b. My superior *frequently* becomes
involved in the job I do. □ 5 4 3 2 1   0   1 2 3 4 5 NA

                                  Pressure   *Satisfaction*

THANK YOU

GENERAL (PHYSICAL) HEALTH QUESTIONNAIRE

(Slightly Adapted Gurin Psychosomatic Symptom List)

Below is a list of different troubles and complaints which people often
have. For each one please tick the column which tells how often you
have felt like this during the last three months.

	I feel like this:			
	A lot	Quite often	Occasionally	Never
1. Do you ever have any trouble getting to sleep or staying asleep?				
2. Have you ever been bothered by nervousness, feeling fidgety or tense?				
3. Are you ever troubled by headaches or pains in the head?				
4. Are there any times when you just don't feel like eating?				
5. Are there times when you get tired very easily?				
6. How often are you bothered by having an upset stomach?				
7. Do you find it difficult to get up in the morning?				
8. Does ill-health ever affect the amount of work you do?				
9. Are you ever bothered by shortness of breath when you are not exercising or working hard?				
10. Do you ever feel 'put out' if something unexpected happens?				

11. Are there times when you tend to cry easily?
12. Have you ever been bothered by your heart beating hard?
13. Do you ever smoke, drink or eat more than you should?
14. Do you ever have spells of dizziness?
15. Are you ever bothered by nightmares?
16. Do your muscles ever tremble enough to bother you (e.g. hands tremble, eyes twitch)?
17. Do you ever feel mentally exhausted and have difficulty in concentrating or thinking clearly?
18. Are you troubled by your hands sweating so that you feel damp and clammy?
19. Have there ever been times when you couldn't take care of things because you just couldn't get going?
20. Do you ever just want to be left alone?

To the remaining questions please answer 'yes' or 'no'

	Yes	No
21. Do you feel you are bothered by all sorts of pains and ailments in different parts of your body?		
22. For the most part do you feel healthy enough to carry out the things you would like to do?		
23. Have you ever felt that you were going to have a nervous breakdown?		
24. Do you have any particular physical or health problem?		

Comparison of 16pf scores to those of 'normative' populations

Factor	Low score description	1. US male population				2. Henly managers				High score description	Factor
		Raw Scores			Study sample	Stern Scores					
		sig	t	US pop		Study sample	Henly	t	sig		
A	Reserved, detached, critical cool (sizothymia)	0.02	2.34	8.52	8.91	A 5.85	6.1 (high)	1.51	NS	Outgoing, warmhearted, easy-going, participating (Affectothymia, formerly cyclothymia)	A
B	Less intelligent, concrete-thinking (Lower scholastic mental capacity)	0.001	16.26	4.34	6.12	B 7.70	8.6 (high)	6.68	0.001	More intelligent, abstract-thinking, bright (Higher scholastic mental capacity)	B
C	Affected by feelings, emotionally less stable, easily upset (Lower ego strength)	0.001	5.46	7.55	8.41	C 6.25	4.9	8.74	0.001	Emotionally stable, faces reality, calm, mature (Higher ego strength)	C
E	Humble, mild, accommodating, conforming (Submissiveness)	0.001	3.37	5.63	6.17	E 5.94	6.1 (high)	1.05	NS	Assertive, independent, aggressive, stubborn (Dominance)	E
F	Sober, prudent, serious, taciturn (Desurgency)	0.001	6.90	6.89	5.65	F 4.48	5.5	6.01	0.001	Happy-go-lucky, impulsively lively, gay, enthusiastic (Surgency)	F
G	Expedient, evades rules feels few obligations (Weaker superego strength)					G				Conscientious, persevering, staid, rule-bound (Stronger superego strength)	G
H	Shy, restrained, diffident, timid (Threctia)	0.01	3.28	7.18	6.60	H 5.12	5.2 (low)	0.51	NS	Venturesome, socially bold, unhibited, spontaneous (Permia)	H
I	Tough-minded, self-reliant, realistic, no-nonsense (Harria)	0.001	4.28	5.54	6.33	I 6.00	5.0	6.16	0.001	Tender-minded, dependent, over-protected, sensitive (Premsia)	I
L	Trusting, adaptable, free of jealousy, easy to get on with (Alaxia)	0.001	7.53	5.33	4.81	L 4.38	5.9	10.10	0.001	Suspicious, self-opinionated, hard to fool (Protension)	L

Factor	Low pole					Factor					Factor	High pole
M	Practical, careful, conventional, regulated by external realities, proper (Praxernia)	0.01	2.59	5.59	6.02	M	5.84	5.2 (high)	3.95	0.001	M	Imaginative, wrapped up in inner urgencies, careless of practical matters, bohemian (Autia)
N	Forthright, natural, artless, sentimental (Artlessness)					N	5.66	5.2 (low)	2.69	0.02	N	Shrewd, calculating, wordly, penetrating (Shrewdness)
O	Placid, self-assured, confident, serene (Untroubled adequacy)	0.01	2.59	5.64	5.11	O					O	Apprehensive, worrying, depressive, troubled (Guilt proneness)
Q_1	Conservative, respecting established ideas, tolerant of traditional difficulties (Conservatism)					Q_1	5.32	5.9	3.29	0.01	Q_1	Experimenting, critical, liberal, analytical, free-thinking (Radicalism)
Q_2	Group-dependent, a 'joiner' and sound follower (Group adherence)	0.001	8.59	4.01	5.61	Q_2	6.78	6.0 (high)	4.60	0.001	Q_2	Self-sufficient, prefers own decisions, resourceful (Self-sufficiency)
Q_3	Undisciplined self-conflict, follows own urges, careless of Protocol (Low integration)	0.001	3.98	7.88	8.48	Q_3					Q_3	Controlled, socially-precise, following self-image (High self-concept control)
Q_4	Relaxed, tranquil, torpid, unfrustrated (Low ergic tension)					Q_4	5.29	5.7	2.47	0.02	Q_4	Tense, frustrated, driven, overwrought (High ergic tension)

Index